For the Ancestors

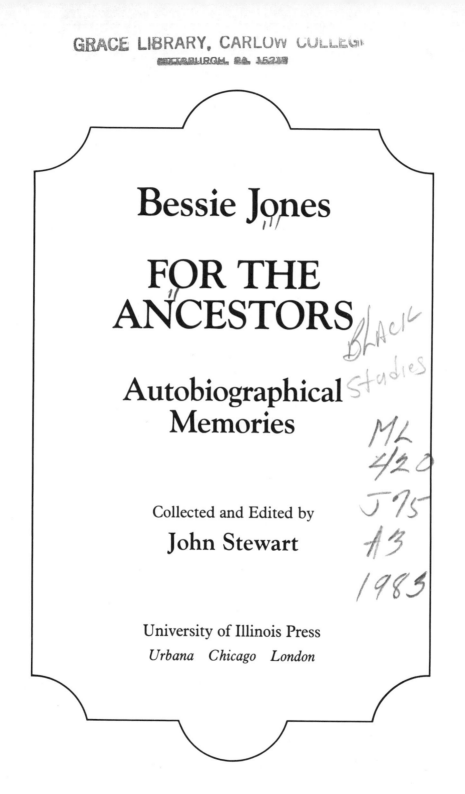

# Bessie Jones

# FOR THE ANCESTORS

## Autobiographical Memories

Collected and Edited by

## John Stewart

University of Illinois Press

*Urbana   Chicago   London*

Library of Congress Cataloging in Publication Data

Jones, Bessie, 1902-
  For the ancestors.

  Bibliography: p.
  1. Jones, Bessie, 1902-    . 2. Singers—United
States—Biography.    I. Stewart, John, 1933-
II. Title.
ML420.J75A3   1983   783.6'7'0924  [B]   82-8593
ISBN 0-252-00959-2                 AACR2

# Contents

# Introduction

AN INTRODUCTION to a work such as this immediately raises a welter of questions and ideas in my mind, not the least of which has to do with the survival of the tradition Bessie Jones has worked so hard to maintain. Such a concern necessarily generates additional thoughts on the processes which seem to affect minority traditions, traditions in the society at large, and beyond that the dialectics linking culture and creativity. Clearly, however, this introduction is not the place to pursue all such questions, and remarks will be limited to those surrounding the potential of the black spiritual tradition so richly depicted in Bessie Jones's life story.

This tradition has its origins in the plantation experience endured by African slaves and their descendants, and any approach to an understanding of its continuity may begin with an examination of these origins. Also, the concern with potential inevitably leads to the problem of process. Therefore, unlike the several excellent historical works which chronicle plantation activities, the focus here will be on tradition as the surviving essence of such activities.

The plantation era was, along with everything else, one of high creativity during which new regional traditions were forged. Cultural elements from wide-ranging areas of the globe were brought together in aggressive frontiers, and patterned into the skills people required for dealing with each other and with the environment within which they sought to improve their existence. How particular cultural elements fared within the milieu of the plantation has been a source of contention for some time, especially in regard to those elements brought in by the Africans, who comprised the under class of slaves without power to impress their culture on others, or indeed defend it among themselves.

Some argue that structurally the plantation was such an enforcing institution that the African slaves had no choice but to submit to the dictates of those who owned and managed them. And it is well known that slave owners throughout the hemisphere generally cultivated a profound antipathy toward African culture—and toward Africans themselves. With no opportunity for forthright self-expression, this argument concludes, slaves developed basic habits of imitating and feigning, to the extent that they became locked into a stage of development analogous to that of children, whose cultural adjustment to their environment is centered on pleasing others.

Another line of argument points to variations within the plantation system itself. Differences between plantations in terms of their size, ownership, geographical location are correlated with different potentials in cultural opportunity among the slaves. It is argued, for instance, that slavery as practiced by Catholics was less pernicious than that practiced by Protestants, or vice versa. Or that island plantations were more benign than those in the continental interiors. It is also frequently pointed out that the African slave community was itself initially multi-cultural, and without the demographic bases required for maintenance and elaboration of an African culture.

Those who disagree point to continuities in various expressive forms—music, lore, and religion, principally—claiming such as evidence that certain African culture traits survived, even thrived, throughout the plantation experience. And lately "the African experience" is increasingly being identified as the core factor in certain regions within the hemisphere.

All of these arguments, most of them of interest to historians, anthropologists, and other scholars only, are occasioned by the greater question: whether the disadvantageous position of blacks in modern American society is directly linked to their having made no significant contribution to the cultural heritage of the society, and further, whether they have the resources to make any such contribution. The arguments and "proofs" occasioned by this question are as much products of a moral imagination as they are assessments of actual history. They give blacks reason to "prove" themselves on one hand, while on the other serve as justification for all in their positive or negative stance toward a black presence. But questions of interpretation aside, there can be no denying that the resettling of the western hemisphere initiated by the Europeans in the sixteenth century occasioned a severe tax on the inventive resources of all involved. And even though the plantation, in its role as the dominant settler form for over three centuries, was fairly static and rigid in structure, within its frame agricultural, social, and expressive experiments and innovations did occur, if for no other reason than to keep the structure itself viable. The process by which such experiments and innovations became custom, and custom eventually law, accompanied as it was by the integration of increasingly complex units—from individual, to class, caste, or social units—was inevitably linked with the evolution of a vision of society.

The reduction of Africans from servants to hereditary chattel during the first half of the seventeenth century is linked with the rapid conversion of the wilderness, an equally rapid increase in the African population, and the integration of society and work in terms of a feudal vision in which Africans and some others were cast as tillers of the soil, and mechanics of the menial, in perpetual service to an agrarian aristocracy. Race, nationality, political and religious affiliation—all played their parts as significant markers in this process, with each category, so defined, fashioning its own internal cohesion, as well as techniques and media of articulation with other categories, as the whole socio-cultural operation carried out its conquest of the new land.

What does all this have to do with the black spiritual tradition? In the first place, this tradition was forged at the heart of the grand conquest, and served as the basis for its success. If Africans had not mastered the techniques of working for nothing in the economic sense, it is very likely that the whole plantation enterprise would have failed. Slavery involved a number of deeply coercive practices; but coercion by itself never sustained a people, nor made them productive. Africans learned to cultivate certain "benefits" from the slave experience quite apart from any the slave masters could have given. And among these was a direct relationship with a spiritual overworld in which they could recognize themselves as stewards of a cosmic heritage. This recognition expressed itself in many ways, the most obvious of which is the repertoire that we call "the spirituals." This repertoire, however, is only part of a system for the construction and interpretation of meaning in all phases of everyday existence, within the terms of what John Gwaltney labels a clandestine theology. When Muhammad Ali thanks Allah, or Mike Weaver The Lord, for bringing victory their way, such expressions are directly in the tradition of a perspective that recognizes spiritual intention as a decisive factor in the outcome of all interactions. The Africans' adaptation of the *terminologies* provided by the plantation for fostering this tradition permitted it to transcend both spatial and temporal constraints, and thus contribute to a necessary level of integrity among the slaves themselves. And beyond the plantation experience this tradition survives still, encouraged to some extent by the caste-like restrictions faced by blacks in the society, but sharing now the status as genitor of rule and meaning.

It is generally agreed that the onset of the modern industrial age and shifts in trade, demographic, and landholding patterns were the factors which led to the decline of the plantation. But it must also be the case that the ossification of methods for carrying out necessary interrelational processes must have made a strong contribution to such decline. Whatever the reason, the plantation as an economic system just became less viable with the onset of industry. Despite this decline of the plantation as an economically viable institution, however, certain of its structural and expressive aspects survive, bearing the properties of a great nostalgia and affective power. This is perhaps evidence that processes, once having achieved integrity, do not voluntarily reverse themselves, even when their factors of sustenance are depleted. But rather that at such depletion, their structural and expressive elements convert into affective resources capable of invoking but not carrying the power to demand certain types of interactions, while the process itself goes on, exploiting new sources of social energy. In any case, among the survivals of all those innovations which evolved within a plantation context, the black spiritual tradition is a dominant one.

From any perspective this tradition has to be seen as syncretic in nature, combining as it does elements from African, European, and Native American sources. But it is unique in the blending and energizing of these elements. And that, despite all the arguments about origins and questions of priority—i.e., are black spirituals an adaptation of a white form, or vice versa?—is the phenomenon of note, evidencing as it does the integrative character of culture. Just as the slaves constructed a unique tradition, from the perspective of the society at large this tradition has to be seen as one in a compendium of traditions which themselves all serve as interrelated complexes in the wider culture. And while it may be very difficult—and in the end pointless—to trace the lineage of elements which comprise any traditional complex, the logic of the process is clear. The question may then be asked, do minor traditions simply disappear once having made their contribution to the grand design?

And if the relationship between minor and grand traditions may be conceptualized in terms of the exchange of energy, it would seem that once absorbed, the minor tradition is separated from a special and committed energy base, and does run the risk of being ultimately depleted or generalized to the extent that it loses a specific profile and power. Such has not been the case with the black spiritual tradition, however. It continues to command significant commitment among black people, and its presence may be felt in contexts as varied as the home, the church, the street corner, the athletic arena, the workplace, the stage, the picket line—wherever black people get together to do things. Apparently people of African descent in America have not come around to placing any great trust in the inheritance of a great Enlightenment which fostered "rational man" and particularly his ability to superimpose his welfare upon the universe. Perhaps the historical experience of racial discrimination and segregation could not permit otherwise. In fact, one of the attitudinal fallouts from this experience is a hardening skepticism, which may well be the significant source of entropy faced by the spiritual tradition. But it survives, and does so not only as a reality for black folk but for whites and others as well. One sees this clearly in the response to root exponents of the tradition.

Regardless of the political naiveté and personal quirks which may have marked the career of Martin Luther King, Jr., he nevertheless could invoke a spiritual communion of enormous intensity. So that within range of his voice even the cynics could not help but be affected. What King achieved at various rostrums and roadsides throughout the country Muhammad Ali achieved in the ring, and Miles Davis and John Coltrane with their horns. And there were countless others before them, many in their wake, and still more to come. In fact, any black street or block or neighborhood has its core carriers who through a combination of devotion and other gifts become source and support for others. Bessie Jones is precisely such a person.

Although "the spirituals" are not widely sung anymore, nor are their secular counterparts—those song-games in which the slaves joined league with the spirit to instruct the slave masters and themselves—these forms are alive and well with and around Bessie Jones. She has been devoted to singing and performing these forms for practically all her adult life. The texts and musical interpretations coded in the spirituals and game songs comprise for her an alphabet of root intelligence that is the minimum and at the same time the all that one needs to conduct a well-realized existence. She believes and communicates this. And it is not only the text and the music that are of consequence, but, as well, the actual lives of the people who initially voiced them. Through these lives the forms were empowered, and through these forms the ancestral reality is transformed into an immediately available power. The forms mediate the distance separating the generations and bring them into immediate contact. In the conviction of this relationship Bessie could in turn give her life to enriching and advancing the tradition—although such a conviction came neither easily nor as a result of her initial life choices. The route to the ancestors courses through the byways of the overworld; and it is only as she was called to membership in that world that the past became affective reality. There she was linked through the ancestors to all creation—a system of relationships that would in turn place her in the future, as she herself became an ancestor.

Like so many others of her generation in Georgia, South Carolina, and other regions of the South, she has maintained that sense of the world as a spiritual domain, and life as a perpetual undertaking in learning and adjusting to the ways of the spirit. The black ancestors understood this, and they were good at it. Their legacy—the songs, sayings, and performances they created—amounts to something of a basic survival kit that people should always have about. Bessie Jones firmly believes this, and through her performances and general advocacy she has made a striking contribution to the survival of this tradition. She understands and appreciates the modern trend of "telling it like it is" among blacks. But while the utility of this style is undeniable on the social plane, she perceives a more profound level, where interaction not with others but with what precedes and will outlast them can be conducted in oblique signs and metaphors only. To lose our skills at this level is tantamount to cutting ourselves off from the prime source of power. The performance of songs and games for which she is nationally known, then, is to her much more than entertainment. It is a gift from the ancestors which she is committed to passing on to those who come after. It is part of the reason why her work has been focused so heavily among children.

Before she settled into being a full-time advocate of "the spirit" Bessie Jones had been a sharecropping farmhand in south central Georgia, a domestic servant in various white homes in Georgia and Florida, and a migrant worker traveling with the crops between Florida and Connecticut. Each of these careers occurred in distinctive milieus with their attendant lifeways. From her memory we get glimpses of what it was like being a migrant laborer, and being a maid in upper-class homes. But the most fully remembered period in Bessie Jones's life includes those formative years when she was a girl and young woman moving with her family from farm town to farm town in central Georgia. Bessie belongs to the second generation of Black Americans born after slavery, those who came along in the teeth of the backlash against the post–Civil War reconstruction, at a time when that glimmer of hope sparked by Abraham Lincoln's emancipation speech had been battened again beneath the round of hardships faced by the unpropertied freemen. At the turn of the century there was little opportunity in Georgia for blacks (or anyone else) to acquire industrial skills. Most Georgians made their living from the land—agriculturally, farming timber, or in the extraction of minerals—and the plantations which had been deconstructed as a result of the Civil War were raised again on wage rather than slave labor, and with techniques designed to keep the wage laborer tied to the soil. Sharecropping and various other forms of tenancy were among the most widespread and successful of these techniques.

In remembering back to that time, Bessie recalls that a distinction was made between renters and sharecroppers, with renters enjoying a greater measure of independence and therefore higher status. Independent behavior by blacks of any status, however, invited tragedy. And she recalls as well the terrifying matter-of-factness with which black families absorbed the lynching. That concubinage, too, which since the days of slavery had ordered sex relations between black females and white males was also a vivid survival during her childhood. So much so that it was accepted as a matter of course, and "nobody much paid any attention to that stuff." On the other hand, relations between black males and white females served as the basis for social violence, and was consequently conducted in a surreptitious manner.

The greater danger, though, lurked in the surrounding spirit world, which included—as it does for many pre-mechanized rural agricultural communities—ghosts, vampires, witches, and various other threatening supernaturals. Beyond the race hatred, human greed, and ignorance that underlay many of the dangers faced on the social plane, these supernaturals were in fact perpetrators of a primordial malevolence, the sole defense against which was a beneficent divine power that could be invoked by formula, and that made itself evident in signs. The knowledge of spiritual formulas and some skill in the interpretation of signs were important early cultural acquisitions. The oppositions which comprised the supernatural world clearly mirrored those encountered in real life, the contest between the devil, his retinue, and the divine savior being of a cast similar to that between the daily exploitation of the social world and an inner generative spirituality. And coping with violations of any order—whether against the body, the mind, or the spirit—involved the oblique expression, which—whether in sex or song—served always to activate the principle of humanity's transcendence over history.

By contrast, in the coastal region which finally came to be Bessie Jones's home, and from where she launched into national prominence, neither sharecropping nor renting emerged as significant forms of tenancy. Blacks on the coast could boast a certain "independence" as part of their heritage coming down from the days of slavery. Popular exegesis holds that plantation owners and their families on the coast, unable to withstand the seasonal lowland miasma, had to cultivate the good graces of their slaves, so their properties would be well looked after while they sat out the dangerous summers in their up-country retreats. This resulted in slaves being left under the supervision of some of their own number. Negro drivers thus acquired responsibility for marshaling the work force, seeing to its needs—insofar as these were provided by the plantation—and maintaining discipline. Such a pattern of control must have included lines of communication between the plantation owners and slaves other than the drivers, as a way of limiting the authority of the drivers themselves. In all it became the basis for an affective form of slave-master relationship.

Owners often granted restricted kin status to some slaves, who in turn expressed their affiliation in diverse ways. The story is told, for instance, of Neptune Small, who went off to the Civil War as body servant to the son of his owner's family. The son was killed during a battle in Virginia. During the night Neptune searched the battlefield until he found the body of the dead soldier, and then brought it all the way back home to St. Simons, where he remained in the service of the family until long after the war. And every worthy published history of Old St. Simons carries an account of "Driver" Morris the negro, who whipped the hundred slaves under his supervision into safety during a hurricane rather than let them take to evacuation from the island by boat. He thus saved their lives—and his master's wealth. When offered his freedom by the plantation owner in return, Morris refused it, accepting instead an inscribed cup. The cup was supposed to be inherited by a male child. Morris had no male child, and he eventually gave the cup to a female member of the planter's family for her boy child.

Such intense affiliation was not the only trope generated by the system of "independence," however. As Margaret Davis Cate notes: "During the Civil War St. Simons was abandoned by the plantation owners. The men were in the Army of the Confederacy and the women and children refugeed on the mainland at Waynesville and later, at Waresboro. The Negro slaves remained on the plantations and many of the men joined the United States Army, enlisting in a regiment commanded by Col. Thomas Wentworth Higginson, the first Negro regiment in the United States Army" (p. 229).

Along with taking care of the plantations, the slaves had not forgotten how to take care of themselves. They were the ones who manned the boats along the inlets, rivers, and sounds that link the coastal islands to the mainland. And they learned well how to be at home on this water, which they called "God's Pantry." Also, despite the fictions of kinship and comparative independence, the reality of the African's true state in America was fixed in local consciousness through the location and memory of Ebo Landing. It was here that several Africans shackled together entered the water and waded in to their deaths rather than undergo life on some plantation. The water brought them, the water would take them back. And in keeping with their origins, the coastal slaves developed an idiosyncratic version of speech, song, religion, lore, and other customs which all came to be known as Gullah. One writer describes Gullah territory as "a haunted land of brooding ghosts, sorcery and superstitions, intricate rituals, and a strange and lyrical language" (Fancher, p. 42). For this same writer Gullah culture was "the customs and superstitions of half a hundred African tribes . . . mingled and renewed to form one of the unique cultures of the United States" (p. 42). Central to this realized version of African culture, and clearly a retention from the old country, was the intense awareness of a spiritual overworld as the place from which men issued, and to which they returned. Gullah culture therefore placed great emphasis on birth and burial ceremonies, and the interpretation of signs as passage between the two extremes was negotiated. There is the notion that Gullah customs carried no significance in the wider coastal society, other than as an expression of ignorance plus an impoverished inheritance. Fancher, however, notes that within Gullah "superstitions are endless, and few white people ignore them" (p. 48), and "the coastal whites seldom question these customs, for they have learned that the Gullahs are in some ways much closer to reality than they are" (p. 49).

When Bessie Jones first visited the coast as a young woman she was struck by the geography—the vast expanses of water— and the overt social integrity among blacks. She was struck by their "independence," and the cadence of their speech. But mostly she was elated to find a widespread ambience for the spiritual tradition in which she had been reared, and especially its strong expression in song. In time she joined the Spiritual Singers Society of Coastal Georgia organized by Lydia Parrish, herself like Bessie Jones an outsider to the coastal region, but one who devoted much of her life to maintenance of the coastal singing tradition. The Spiritual Singers Society, organized in the early 1930s was Lydia Parrish's way "to help restore the prestige which the slave songs once enjoyed."

At the end of the plantation era following the Civil War, not only had the production systems of the coastal plantations been dismantled, but the folk culture which had energized those systems lost, in a sense, its raison d'être. The lumber mills and tourist industry, which replaced the plantations as the dominant economic enterprises, introduced new people with different attitudes, and engendered a different quality of relationship between the total work force and the environment, as well as between blacks, whites, and other categories within that work force. So that Lydia Parrish could write: "When I arrived on St. Simon's in 1912, the stillness of the Negroes was puzzling until questioning brought out the fact that the island was a summer resort, and contact with city whites and their black servants had had its numbing influence; that the old-time singing had gone out of style, and spirituals weren't sung any more" (p. 9). Of course it was not simply the contact between coastal blacks and city folk that was responsible for the "stillness" that puzzled Lydia Parrish. It was the passing of a whole way of life. While the end of slavery may have done no more than take away (temporarily) the substantial motivation for relying on the spirit, the new economic order introduced elements that found their sanction in a total negation of the spiritual.

Lydia Parrish chose to combat this negation. For her, the slave songs "may have resulted from a spark of divine fire," with blacks, "like so much tinder," carrying them far and wide "through the agency of the slave markets or the removal of the planters from one state to another," (p. 5). A justification of her own role as a member of the distributive agency notwithstanding, it is interesting to note that in organizing her society she would draw on "singing families" who "appeared to have inherited the gift." For actually, *inheritance* in this case involves more than basic biology. A set of attitudes, texts, and performance skills are all part of an inheritance within the framework of domestic culture. The family has ever been a unit for challenging time, not only in the preservation of blood but in the presentation of culture as well. Bessie Jones's story gives a sparkling illustration of this.

She remembers with love and gratitude the grandfathers, uncles, and others who taught her the song-games and the lore she can recite, and from whom she learned the style that makes her performance distinctive. It was by accident, not design, that she met the father of her first child, who was himself a member of a singing family. Their union, however, resulted in her leaving inland Georgia for the coast, where her background made it easy for his family to invite her to sing with them. That led to her joining Lydia Parrish's society, to eventual "discovery" by Alan Lomax, and to national recognition. As the leading active singer in the Georgia Sea Island tradition, she brought members of her family into the group, all of whom—especially the grandchildren—have been reared in a relationship with her similar to the one she had with her grandfather. And now that she is less able to be a constant leader, Douglas and Frankie Quimby—parents to one set of her grandchildren—have stepped in to share the role. The survival of tradition is clearly linked to the relationship between kinship and performance, and the Bessie Jones story in this regard is representative of a more general pattern in which root exponents serve as conductors of a tradition. But perhaps more cogently than others, she exemplifies and articulates the meaning of this role for those whom it chooses.

In this reconstructed account of her life a constant dialog between the self of her ideal person and her functional selves is revealed. And mirrored in that dialog is the tension between her inheritance and her contribution. She has set a standard which requires that she contribute no less than what she received from the ancestors, and, as is perhaps inevitable, moments when it appears that this is not being the case are troublesome. The best evidence of success in this regard would of course be seeing the inheritance at work in the children. This has not happened to her satisfaction, and that is why at age eighty Bessie Jones still goes by road (not train, and never by plane) to wherever opportunity is provided for her to perform and teach the ring games and songs and elaborate on their meanings before an audience. And in telling this story of her life, which constitutes on one level a statement in the continuing dialog with her ideal—her aim is to be teacher by illustrated example, and in a way less contained by time than are her personal appearances. Therefore, while her story acknowledges her debt to the ancestors, it is told also for the young ones, who will, it is hoped, come to benefit from the tradition she passes on, and will in turn themselves strive to maintain it. It is told for others, too, the patrons and organizers who have contributed to the survival of the tradition from its periphery.

## Working with Bessie Jones

It is left now for me to say something about the construction of this text. It is a narrative built around the principal events in the life of Bessie Jones that relate to how she and I perceived her at the time the oral version was collected. It was subtly but clearly understood, then, that there were some things about which she would not speak, some things which would be told as private explanatory accounts not to appear as parts of the published narrative. These are much like the scaffolding that holds things together and permits access while the carpenter does his work but is then stripped away to reveal the finished structure. In some ways this scaffolding was as interesting as, or even more so than, the finished structure (consider the scaffolding for the great pyramids, if they used scaffolds) for the qualities which it introduced into our relationship. As the rapport required for the oral work came to be established, I was viewed both as cultural filiate and other. The fact that I was born and reared outside the United States, that my speech had a non-U.S. accent to it, that I was a university person—all were elements of my difference. On the other hand, the fact that I am black, and familiar to some extent with coastal black culture, identified me as affiliate. Also, our interests coincided on the need for this work to be done. Bessie Jones had been awaiting the opportunity to tell this version of her life story. It was her wish to leave such a work as part of her legacy. I was interested in the lore and other details of her biography as contribution to the ethno-history of black Americans. The idea of recording the life story of Bessie Jones came out of conversations in Illinois with Douglas and Frankie Quimby, who are her kin and are themselves members of the Georgia Sea Island Singers. I traveled to St. Simons for the first time in May of 1977 and met Bessie Jones at her home—a little house on Proctor Lane surrounded by towering oaks, and with a perpetual light (gas) burning in the front yard. My plan was to record her dictation of her life story, follow that with interviews among others who know her, then do the necessary geographical and archival research and myself prepare a biography.

It was not difficult meeting Bessie Jones, nor did it require much on my part to have her agree to my taping an oral account of her life. There was much that she wanted to say. And more than that, she rapidly deciphered certain signs (I found out later) which indicated that I had been appropriated and sent by the greater process out of which this autobiography would come. She introduced me readily to her relatives and neighbors, and within the first two days we settled into a routine in which we spent from mid-morning to mid-afternoon taping, and the rest of some afternoons visiting. We worked like this for the next two weeks, sometimes at her home, other times at the motel where I was staying.

After the second or third day of taping, however, it became clear that I was not going to get the sort of sober "dictation" I had imagined. Her tellings of past times and events was as much the dramatization of a philosophy as it was the recounting of any sequence of experience. She had observations to make on the daily news, or about chance encounters, which would stimulate memories cross-cutting many years and relationships. She required a chorus, and asked my opinions, and our "dictation" would easily slip into dialog.

Through it all there was an unmistakable mystical force associated with her presence, a force much more easily felt than explained. Whether we were talking about the personalities and habits of spirits ("Sometimes all they want is a little attention"), or the peculiarities of life in a sharecropper's cabin ("On hot days Momma soaked sheets and quilts and hung them inside to cool off the house"), or having a discussion of change on St. Simons ("Many old blacks mortgaged their inheritance on cheap loans and drinks to ———, and that's how they lost their land"), Bessie Jones was open and full of information and the insistence that holiness is the greatest principle. She seemed attuned to this island where tall brooding trees hung with moss spread deep shadows everywhere, and seemed to emanate from herself a sort of subterranean knowledge which though verbally mute could flash in a look as sharply as sunlight glancing off interior foliage. I had, of course, been set up by the geography, and could only later on record:

> At first view, these islands do reflect a golden aura, by virtue of the broad, pale-yellow marshes which separate them from the mainland. And there is a magical aspect as one crosses the marsh to enter in between the great oaks draped with hanging moss, the pines, that dominate the natural vegetation of the coastal region. But it is not the same magic of those islands farther south—Puerto Rico, Jamaica, Guadeloupe, St. Martin—where sharp mountains inevitably pull the vision skyward, and the firmament and ocean cup the sun's sparkle. It is warm, here in Georgia, but the waters are not blue, and there are no hills to sound back in echo the fear, joy, or other palpitations of a collective heart. This is not a land of the drum. The rhythm here is muted, one-dimensional, flat as that of the broken waves. The water does not speak in many voices. In fact, it speaks hardly at all above a controlled murmur. The magic of Georgia's Golden Isles is not one of lurking transport or malevolence, it is simply one of agony. It is the mute charge of African slaves who were denied so much, they finally learned how to speak without saying; it is the fascinated arrest of others who didn't intend for things to turn out the way they did dreaming through the results of a miscalculation.

Invariably there were two of Bessie Jones's great-grandchildren with us while we worked, and often after taping we all rode around in my car as they taught me the geography of St. Simons Island and certain neighborhoods in Brunswick. Such rides were often punctuated by lunch stops, snack stops, and spontaneous visits to the homes of various friends and relatives, particularly the homes of Doug and Frankie Quimby. When Bessie Jones needed to withdraw and rest, or when there were others whom she had to see, I spent time with the Quimbys. They were great hosts themselves, often serving meals at dinnertime, and taking me along with them to church and other ceremonies where Doug, who is a gospel singer as well as a lead with the Georgia Sea Island Singers, performed. This widened the circle of people I met and took me rapidly to an intimate view of the religious

culture among blacks in St. Simons, Brunswick, and some neighboring towns.

I found it at first extraordinary, the degree to which religion
pervaded the lives of young and old, male and female. Then it
quickly became no longer extraordinary. It was something I had
known in earlier years of my life and forgotten. When time came
for me to leave and return to Illinois, those closed-off memories
from that earlier time had all but completely surfaced, and I knew
I would come again to the Georgia coast, intrigued to see how
my self would deal with this resurrected version of its previous
history. I would come again, too, because although Bessie Jones
talked freely enough about many things, there were others she
hardly touched on at all. Understandably, she was constructing a
text by which she wished to be remembered—not necessarily
reconstructing the actual record of her life. It is the limitation of
all autobiography. So I would come again to probe respectfully,
and sit through the hours of oblique dialog in which certain
truths about ourselves slowly make their appearance. I would
come again because the work required it. But "the work" involved more than giving Bessie Jones a reason and the opportunity to speak. It also involved getting on with whatever was to be
the outcome of my own awakening.

My second visit to the Georgia coast began in late July, 1977.
The routine with Bessie Jones picked up where we had left off,
and I had time to interview other people, read at the public
libraries on St. Simons and in Brunswick, gather documents,
visit Jekyll and Sapelo islands and various inland towns west to
the Alabama border. These were good ways to elaborate both the
historical and geographical context in which Bessie's story was
set and my own was to evolve.

I did not stay in a motel this time, but in a home located
between the racially segregated graveyards in Brunswick. This
invited some personal attention which was not all comfortable.
But I can say that my own story developed to a very satisfying
resolution, for which this work is the evidence.

When the time came for us to visit Dawson and neighboring
communities of Bessie Jones's childhood, I grew nervous. That

was the week during which the "Dawson Five" were being tried, and there was news that the citizens were restive at the inflow of outsiders attracted by the trial. But Bessie was ebullient. She had not been to Dawson in many years, and this trip was an excursion for her back to that part of the land where she had run across the fields to school, had played "maypop," had learned her children's games and storytelling. She called ahead and arranged for us to stay with a relative in Dawson, and the trip went off without problems.

While in Dawson we stopped by the old "Dillard Place," where the buildings are now overgrown ruins. The old school/church was torn down, but the railway still ran in the same place. We stopped in at the library in town, a place into which Bessie would not have been allowed when she was a child, but yes, the head librarian knew of her and had on the shelf an earlier book co-authored by Bessie (*Step It Down*, Harper & Row), and she wanted her to autograph it and also to come back later during the fall for a concert. It was a good trip for Bessie. And before we left to return to St. Simons, we went around the countryside about Dawson so she could collect some herbs, red dirt, and chalk, which are not to be found on the island.

During the third week in August, 1977, the St. Simons folk festival known from the days of Lydia Parrish was revived, under the auspices of the National Endowment for the Arts and the Glynn County Parks and Recreation Department. Bessie Jones was the center of attraction at this festival, and ABC New York sent a television crew especially to film her onstage leading the Georgia Sea Island Singers. If one needed evidence of the potency of black spiritual song, here it was. For two days crowds came to listen and join in the chanting of both the old and new, the spiritual and the gospel. Some among the young preferred the gospel, but it was clear that the spirituals remain unparalleled in their vision of an ironic universe in which all things are inevitably bound to their contradictions. It was a good festival, and I filmed much of what took place there.

The last tapes were made in January of 1978, when I visited on the coast for three weeks. This time I stayed at a motel and all the taping was done there. On this occasion I had a transcribed draft from the earlier tapes and we went over it together, settling questions of detail and development. Bessie was her usual affable and outspoken self, and she arranged for me to visit the private plantation where the Georgia Sea Island Singers continue still to entertain by performing the old plantation repertoire.

It was good working with Bessie Jones. She was at times mildly calculating, requiring to be entertained by befuddlement on my part. At other times we were together, in a tacit conspiracy to befuddle others. This marked the wish for both revelation and avoidance of disrespectful exposure which no field worker ought to dishonor. She had some advice for me from time to time, and in a way her preception of what she might give me had some influence on how she revealed things about herself. Working with and observing her put me in touch not only with a grand lady, but also with inner reaches of myself that might otherwise have gone unawakened. And for that I am thankful.

I am also indebted to several other people who made important contributions toward the completion of this work. Douglas and Frankie Quimby, George Cohen, Genoa Martin, Lula Butler, Earl Hill were among the first people to make me welcome in Glynn County and share their time, homes, and other resources with me. Mary Brown patiently typed the initial transcriptions, and Terri Sears the first-draft manuscript. The final manuscript was typed by secretaries of the Social Science Department at the Institute for Advanced Study at Princeton. Institutional assistance also came from the Afro-American Studies and Research Program at the University of Illinois at Urbana, and from the National Endowment for the Arts—the Creative Writing Program. Most of all I am indebted to my wife, Sandra, who coped with my long absences from the family while the taping and other field work proceeded, and who later gave unreservedly of her editorial skills in the preparation of the final manuscript.

John Stewart
*Urbana, 1982*

For the Ancestors

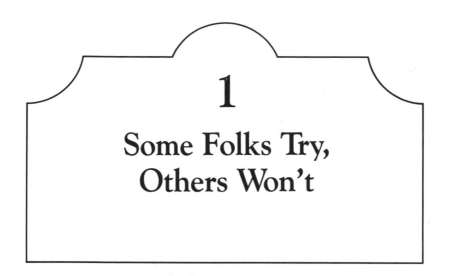

# 1

# Some Folks Try, Others Won't

I WAS BORN in Smithville, Georgia, on February 8th, 1902. My mother never had any other children, and I grew up an only child. My mother was born in a place called Preston, Georgia, not far from Americus, and she was brought up in Buena Vista, Georgia. Her grandmother, which is her mother's mother, she stayed there. My mother had a long name—Abby Lou Frances. At home up around Buena Vista they called her Abby. But down here on the coast they called her Miss Frances. Now Abby, that's God's name. Like my own name. They call me Bessie but that ain't my name. Some people even call me Lizzie, and when they do I won't answer because I want to forget it. My momma always called me Bess which—that is my name. Folks put the Bess-ie to it after we came down to Fitzgerald. It started right down in there. I didn't never want to be called that, and I had a great reason why, but God fixed it like he wanted to and that's the whole name now everywhere—Bessie. But my name is Mary Elizabeth, and I'm named after Momma's mother and Momma's grandma. Momma's mother was named Elizabeth, and her grandmother Mary. I'm named after both of them.

Now I don't know if Mary had any husband or not, but Elizabeth, she didn't have one. She had eight children, though, and I remember some of them. I remember Aunt Evaline, and Lute-

3

cia, and Robert—the one they called Son that got lynched—
Momma, and I don't remember the rest of them. My mother
before she married went by the name of Roberts, but she was a
Green. There was a man named Bill Green—they just called him
Green—he was the daddy of Momma and Uncle Robert; but I
don't know who the daddy for the rest of my grandmother's
children were. Uncle Henry Green, he was half-brother to them
by my father.

Elizabeth, my grandmother, never was married. She never did
marry, but she had her share of children. My momma say I took
after her, 'cause I didn't never want to marry. Never wanted to
marry. I didn't prefer marrying. My momma say that's the way
her mother was. Say she didn't look for no marriage at all. She
had her freedom. And then when she had it, she finished righteous. Told them, say, "You see where God don't care nothing
about that little stuff you do?" Told them what time she was
going, and she was leaving that evening at three o'clock, and just
before she died she was singing a song about get on board li'l
chillun.

Momma said they stayed around that bed trying to watch her,
trying to keep her from going to doing something like that; and,
say, then there was just a certain sound—I've seen that happen
and I been to places where that happen—like something fall
somewhere. And everybody looked around, looked back and she's
gone. Ain't that something?

You see, the Lord don't care nothing about that stuff. What
I'm saying is that all those things like that didn't send my grandmother to hell 'cause she didn't marry a man. She raised her
chillun, she did them well. She brought them up well, sure thing.
So I would've thought that too. I could raise my chillun, and I
couldn't raise my man, see. I don't think I ever would have
married if I hadn't wanted to go on and live for the Lord. That's
the only way, because I wasn't ready to marry anybody. But I
wanted to live for the Lord, and I knew since I was a singer, and
being the way I am with people, friendly people, they would
accuse me of every man that came by. I didn't want to be slurred
all the time, so I thought I better go ahead and get my own

husband. That's the only reason I married, and that's the truth. Course I liked him alright, but I wouldn't have married him. I would have just gone on. But after you've decided to live your life in the church, and you're a grown woman, you need your own husband.

My grandmother and all of them were farm workers. All of them were—my grandmother, and my great-grand too. And they worked in white people's houses too, you know, like when there wasn't no work out in the fields and things like that for them to do. But they mostly stayed near the cities from where they'd go out and work, rather than stay on the plantations. Momma say most all the black folks stayed in Buena Vista or in Smithville, or Americus. They stayed in the town—what they called inside the city limits—but they worked out in the country. People used to come or send wagons into town to get them. They hoed cotton, and were called hoe-hands. They went and came back every day.

I used to do that too, in Milan, when I stayed in the town part. I had to go out and come in. I reckon I got a whole lot of that and more from my grandmother. I don't like to stay too far away from town. I don't like living in the sticks. I love it for going out there, and think it's a glorious thing to go way out there in the sticks to see people. Way out in the country, oh, it's beautiful. Yards, and chickens walking, and they so free out there, but at night when I want to go to the store, then I don't want to be so far away from it. I may want to go to a drugstore if somebody get sick or something and I don't want to be so far away from it. And when I want to leave there, I don't want to be so far from the train or bus. See, that's just the way it is. I never want to be too far off from town that I can't walk there. And that's just why Momma said that I took all that after her momma. When they be living like that Momma and them wouldn't be living in their own house, they'd be renting.

My great-grandmother, where she stayed at in Smithville, where I was born, that was their home. That was given to them from the background of slavery. Aunt Lilla, my grandmother Elizabeth's oldest child, was begot in slavery but born in freedom. My momma was staying with her in Buena Vista when it came out

5

she was pregnant with me, and Lilla sent her away. Lilla was half white. Up in Buena Vista there's still a grave there, the man's grave who was her daddy. Momma and them showed it to me over and again. He never did deny her, Aunt Lilla. He didn't have to. No such thing then, 'cause didn't nobody take up too much time with it. They didn't worry with it like they did later on up. Later on up they got to be slurring, and it worsened. But he didn't never deny her. And so that's how my great-grandmother had this home. He give her a place to stay in Smithville, and Lilla sent Momma down there so Momma could birth me. Lilla was married to this big shot and she didn't want Momma up there with her. But Lilla wasn't thinking about how she was born. See, that's what made Momma mad. Lilla wasn't thinking about how she was born and she was half white and everything. Thought Momma was going to ruin her house. She couldn't see into it. That's why they say, you looking way over yonder you see, and yet can't see what's happening in your own face. That's right. In the old days they seen it that way.

Momma was brought up up there around Buena Vista. My grandmother Elizabeth had done passed, after which she went to stay with Lilla. Aunt Lil was married—her married name was Evans—and so Momma said when she inspired with me that was a scandal in Lil's home. That's why Momma say she didn't care whether she went to see Aunt Lilla or not after I was born. She didn't go back to see her until I was eight years old. Anyway, I was born down there in Smithville, out of wedlock but come into wedlock. My mother say she carried me down to Dawson when I was seven months. That's how I come to be in Dawson; because she remained there.

Uncle Gene—his name was Eugene Reese—he was my momma's granduncle. Her grandmother's brother. He was already down there in that part of the country around Dawson and Cuthbert, Georgia. There were a great family of us down there and Uncle Gene, I sing a lot of his songs. When he knew this baby was born, which was me, and it was in his momma's house, he knew his momma was old so he decided to let my momma come down and live with him. That's how come Momma went down to Dawson after I was born. She was there about three weeks when she run into James Sampson, who I call Daddy. She run into him and he married her there. Momma stayed with him a long, long time. So I was brought up with that and that's how Jet Sampson came to be my grandfather.

My real father was Ronnie Smith, but James Sampson was the man I call Poppa. That's right. I sure say it that way, and his people after a while considered me nothing but their own child. Some of them up to today don't know there's a difference. The older ones do, but the younger ones that come along, they don't know the difference. But I know the difference.

My real daddy's name was Ronnie Smith—Momma say his name was Joe Ronnie, but nobody quite call him that. His daddy's name was Tom and his momma's name was Molly. She was an Owens before she married. And he had two brothers—John Smith and Coot Smith—and one sister, Hattie, who we used to call Aunt Nen. We used to call Coot Uncle Tunk. They were farming people too. My grandfather, old man Tom Smith—I called him Uncle Tom, but he was my grandpa—I stayed with his family, in and out, and used to tend my auntie's little boy. The older Smiths, they know I'm theirs, but them that I was brought up with didn't know the difference—that Poppa Sampson wasn't my real poppa. It's like that story about the woman who said to her child, "Your daddy ain't your daddy, nohow." But they treat me so good, if they had never told me, I would have never known the difference. And I'm glad they told me.

There are some people in Brunswick who're relatives to the Smiths. Their name is Battle. Two brothers. They're first cousins to my real daddy. Now the Owens were my daddy's mother's people on her side before she married Uncle Tom. But I don't know any of them. All I know is she was an Owens. But I remember their background, and they grew up in the same country as we did. They were light-skinned, all of them that I had seen. My grandmother's hair was so soft til the hairpins would fall out of it. She was part Indian, and real heavy-built. Now I talk just like her. I know I do 'cause I remember how she sound. She used to stammer and I stammer. I remember her voice—talk like she was talking through her nose or something. So I got something from my grandmothers on both sides.

Now on the Smiths' side, Uncle Tom was a shoemaker. He had a real machine, the whole machine that spins and all that, just like a regular shoe place. He made shoes for whites and coloreds alike. He made them for stores and things. He made them right out there from Dawson. I don't know what become of that stuff after we left from up there, but Uncle Tom made shoes, and he used to make all Momma's shoes. My mother was bowlegged, and he told her one day, say, "I'm gonna make you some shoes and you run 'em over you just gon lay down. You gon fall down in 'em." And he made them. He used to call them spool-bottom, 'cause they were wide at the bottom and narrow as they come up. They were cute little shoes. Momma wore them, and she didn't run them over. Now I'm that way. I can run over the stocking part of any shoe after a little while. And so that's what Uncle Tom used to do—sew shoes. He'd make patent-leathers, boots, regular shoes, and whites and coloreds were there, and there wasn't no discrimination with him. They'd come and get them by the oodles, 'cause they were cheap, I guess. But anyhow, he sat there rainy days and nights and made shoes. And then he had his farm, too, and had a cane mill out there. All the families had cane mills, 'cause we made our own syrup and our own brown sugar. They had their own chickens and gardens, too.

Uncle Gene was a carpenter and a farmer. He could make his own things around there, and he never was a sharecropper. He leased his land, and whatever he made he got it, see, and therefore he kept money in the bank. They didn't like that big black nigger in many places. And he was a big black one, too. My son Joe looks something like him. Uncle Gene was dicty, gray-dark, and neat. But he didn't have luck with women. He married seven times. The last wife killed him. The other six died. He killed them, I guess.

I remember he married one woman called Miss Laura Butts. He married her like the fourth Sunday in this month, and the fourth Sunday the next month he buried her. She had cancer and she knowed she did, yet she felt they were giving her somebody to help her. That's all that was. She had cancer of the breast and he put her in the hospital but she was too far gone. And Momma say, "If you quit marrying them old half-dead women, you be alright," but see, he wouldn't marry a black woman. Oh no. His woman had to be real yellow or near about half white, or something. Yes sir. And he was slick black. Really black. He had pretty black hair, and stepped real proud. He could put on a linen-tail white shirt with cuffs—they used to wear cuffs in those days—and them things be near 'bout as white that evening as they were that morning. He was real dicty. Always in his collar and tie.

He used to tell Momma, say, "Well Jack"—he call my momma Jack—"the reason why I don't want to marry no black woman, I don't want in the night we're sleeping and she say, 'Mr. Reese, git off my head.' I want her to say 'Mr. Reese, get off my hair.'" I've seen him say it a many a time. But all of us liked him, and he treated us all good. He say he didn't want nobody the same color as his hair. Too black, they would be, if they the same color as his hair. Old Uncle Gene was a sight. But he was good to people. He was a pretty good carpenter. And he could pick a guitar til he got ready to stop. I mean he was a guitar player. He used to git Aunt Louisianna to come back to him when she quit him with nothing but his guitar. Wouldn't even ask her to go home. Just go where she was staying and stand on the steps or stand out by the gatepost and play that guitar. And Louisianna would get a little embarrassed and here she comes. He'd sing a song and when he looked back and seen her, he didn't ask her where she was going; he didn't ask her anything. They'd just go to walking off and he continued playing and she go to walking behind like a little bitty. Take them to tell you 'bout it! They'd laugh and Louisianna would say, "I declare, I had to go home with that man; he sing so mournful!" They laughed about it theirselves. Yes sir, he could play that guitar. Play what you call them reels and rags. Oh boy, they're so sad. He knowed how to pick it. And that woman had a pretty shape. Real pretty legs. And could she dance! That was the time when they used to have frolics, Grandpa and the others.

Uncle Gene didn't have any children with his first six wives, but the last lady he married, they had a girl, Lula, and a boy. This last wife, we called her Aunt Chery, her mother was Aunt Margaret who Lula and me called Grandma, but she was not my grandmother. She was Lula's grandmother. Aunt Chery had an older child who I used to call Auntie. Uncle Gene was not her father, although he raised her. Reason I call her Auntie is, she and my momma married two brothers. Momma married to Poppa and Auntie married to Nehemiah, all of them Sampsons. In those days, everybody knew they were going to have to call the older ladies Grandma or Auntie, either one . . . but Aunt Margaret who Lula and me called Grandma, she was a witch. For a while we stayed near to them in Bronwood, Georgia, and that's where I found out she was a witch. But I'll get back to that.

Later on Uncle Gene died in Bronwood. He came to be saved; he came to be a deacon in the Holiness Church, sanctified after all them wives he married. He killed off all those women, but after the doctor examined him they said the reason why most of his wives died was he had a white liver. You know, a man that's got a white liver, his women don't live long. He'd kill a heap of them. That's right. You mess with something and some people can make you sick. Something wrong with them that don't agree with you, see. After his fourth wife died they did begin to suspect something was wrong with him, and they examined him and began doctoring on him in Dawson and in Bronwood too. Doctor Ward, I think it was. But there ain't no cure for it. There's a treatment helps the bloodstream in some kind of a way where it won't kill the person with white liver, but other than that it would kill other people when they have connections with them. And Uncle Gene always looked like he was in pretty good health, the shape of him. He didn't look to be sick but that's what he had, and they call it white liver. I don't know if the liver be white or just the blood be white. But it's the blood that kills. 'Cause, they say, when you have connections the blood come through there.

I haven't seen Lula nor her brother in a long while, but I understand that the boy's still in Bronwood and I sure would like to see him. Lula's down in Florida, the last time I heard from her. She had fourteen children, she did. She married a boy I used to be scared of when I was in school, that Taylor boy. They all scattered out and I don't know where they're all at now, but I know that they're close to me. Some of them I don't want to be worried with because they got wrong habits that I don't like. But if I ever do see them or if they come, I have to treat them good.

Uncle Tom, my granddaddy, he didn't never in his life to my knowledge have to go out and buy meat. On the Sampson side they didn't have to go buy any meat either. If they wanted meat in July they went out and killed a hog. That's when they wanted fresh meat. They'd take and kill him in July—it wouldn't make any difference. They were smart. They always raised their own meat. They were very smart in keeping something or other, that's why I could tell folks I've never known what hungry is. A lot of chilluns and a lot of persons can say they suffer. But Uncle Tom and Ma and Pa and them—they were always friends—they had the habit of going and helping a person if he was mistreating his chillun or couldn't feed his chillun or down sick, or something of the kind. There were some men in those days—a lot of men— who just wouldn't do right. They'd know they weren't making nothing, ain't got nothing, and the chillun suffering, yet they didn't want the chillun to ask nobody for nothing. A lot of that was around Dawson. We knew some women to be so low-down and hungry till they couldn't nurse the baby. Didn't have milk. We had to slip food to them and they had to slip and ask for it. . . . "He'll git mad if I ask anybody for anything. He'll git real mad . . ." you see. That little nothing he bringing in, and then trying to go with other women off on the side too, but "Don't ask nobody for nothing"! Just as sure as you're born we used to help them.

You know in those days they used to say you do something to a white person and what will happen to you. With Uncle Gene, Mr. Smith—that's my real daddy—and Aunt Nen, you just have to do it. You just have to do it 'cause they'd sure tell you. You couldn't get too white for them, on the job or anything. They'd tell you right away, "I'm not gonna help you no more" or "You ain't pay me and I ain't gon work." That's all. And they ain't joking. They wouldn't be bothered. They just tell it like it is, that's all. Aunt Nen was working with a white lady in Buena Vista and the woman had fourteen dollars for Aunt Nen—which was a lot of money in those days—and she wouldn't pay Aunt Nen. I'll never forget it. The woman owed her fourteen dollars and she hadn't paid her. Alright. Aunt Nen left home that day— she was there in Dawson—she say, "Momma, I'm going back and git my money." I remember her momma, Aunt Molly—that's my grandmother—she say, "Nen, let her alone." She say, "If she don't pay you God will pay you. Let her alone," standing on the front porch. Aunt Nen say, "I'm gonna git my money from that woman or die." Standing there she say, "She ain't gonna treat me like that." Alright. She started walking to Bronwood to catch the train, and two white men came up in a buggy and asked her if she wanted a ride. She had about a mile to go so she got in the buggy with them. Uncle Tom went on behind her. He was going to see if he could talk her into coming back. Uncle Tom went behind her and he say when he got there the train was pulling off. See, Tom was in bed when they went to git him and he had to git on his clothes and stuff and by the time he got there and everything she was gone.

Later on we heard about Aunt Nen—they had her in jail. Yeah, they had her in Bronwood jail alright, but it didn't cost nothing to get out. The part about it, the white man was at the house when Aunt Nen and his wife got into it about the money. And this was sort of unusual but they say it wasn't nothing to it; he just was that way. Anyhow, he heard them. God come in there some kind of way. The white woman say she wasn't gonna pay Aunt Nen nothing, and all kinds of things. But anyhow, he say he didn't like the way his wife was talking, and just as he was going to go in and tell Aunt Nen that he would pay her, that time they tied up woman for woman. They had one of them wood-burning stoves and Nen turned that woman over on that stove. The woman had long hair, and when Nen grabbed her and turned her over that stove her hair just burnt out. She was hollering and everything. That's when the man went and took Nen off her.

That hair never did come back but that didn't cost Nen one

cent. Uncle Tom went down there and stayed down there with them and got her out. Next week she was home and she had her money. Yeah, that man gave her the money. And the woman had to work on that head, you know, and the hair never did come back there no more. The woman had two children—course they weren't there at the time—and Nen used to wash, iron, and cook for all of them, and that was fourteen dollars a month. I've seen the time and place where Nen would've gone around cursing and carrying on like that they'da beat her to death. That's right. They'da killed her. But that was her own raised home; they all born and raised right there so they knew how it was.

Poppa's family came into Georgia from Virginia right after slavery time. There was Uncle Sam—he was the oldest brother, I think—and Uncle Jesse. They were brothers to Poppa and his sister Aunt Mattie. Jet Sampson—he was the one who mostly brought me up—their daddy, he was married to Julia. Uncle Sam, after freedom, he never lived with anybody. He never did live on no farm or nothing; he just lived in the woods. He worked in the fields and like from time to time to make a little money, but he stayed on the side of the creeks in huts, and mostly made medicine and belts out of snake hides. He was a snake-catcher. When he got free he just meant it to be that way—free—and he never did hitch to nobody. That was Uncle Sam, and they called him a root man. I don't know whether it was or not, but he was very funny. Different.

I remember the last time being in his presence we were going fishing. He lived down on the creek in a hut. When I looked in that little hut there was a couch in there and fireplace—fireplace outside too—and he didn't bother nobody. He just stayed there and sold hides and brung hides to town. That day he cooked fried rattlesnakes and Pa ate some and didn't know it. When he told him, Pa tried to spit and spit and we knew then so we didn't eat none. But Pa had a plenty. I was little, about eight or nine years old right then when Uncle Sam was staying there. And they were talking 'bout how Uncle Sam could be walking just like from one side of the road to the next and they say we're gonna watch and see how he go. And you look off and watch, and look back and you don't see Uncle Sam. It was something to him. He was a little different or at least he made it look like it. But Pa say he believe Uncle Sam sold himself to the devil. I don't know. He never did hurt anybody, but back in those times didn't nobody mess with him either. That's the main thing. I really don't know how he died, but I heard that he died and they buried him in Calhoun, Georgia.

My grandfather and them, they made corn whiskey at the house but they didn't drink any young whiskey. They let it age in a keg in a crib or out in the barn or wherever. And in those days they drank the natural-born wine. They drank that wine and it had to be at least three years of age but it was mostly five— blackberry wine, scuppernong wine, huckleberry wine, plum wine. They usually put it up to age. Whiskey in the whiskey kegs and wine in the wine kegs. Yes, they made their own whiskey right there in the house but they didn't drink that. They called it raw whiskey. Some of the people around the neighborhood didn't make whiskey, but if they knew that you kept it they would send for a gallon or a quart from you and have some of it as medicine for the school chillun. Every one of us had to have a tot in the morning before we went to school. See, we walked to school and it was cold—the ground froze—and they'd give us a half-cup of warm water with a little whiskey and sugar in it and you drank that and went on to school. All the chillun around the neighborhood where I lived. They called it toddy, and we drank it down.

We used to raise our own hogs, and smoked our own meat. We'd go out there and get that oak bark from the trees, then pine tar the meat—that's what makes it taste so good—and smoke it right in the smokehouse. We made our own sausage, too. Sometimes we had it in a bag; sometimes we'd take the gut. You get the little gut of the hog and scrape it clean—it'd be dirty with lining—scrape it until it got thin, then you'd wash it out good. Then you'd grind your meat and season it and you'd stuff it in there. You grind the meat in a meat grinder and then you get a stuffer—something shaped like a coffeepot, large on the top and pointed at the other end—and you put the meat in there and you run the gut up on the stuffer and mash the meat right in there.

Then if you want to make links you just twist it and keep on going.

I used to be the one who would season. Many times people would come and ask Momma and I would go from one pantry to the next seasoning sausages. Because, see, pepper and onions don't bother me. Pepper makes some folks cry and sneeze and everything but they never worried me—and still don't. So I would wash up my little hands and make up them sausages. People would parch their red pepper, then I could break it up and that never worried me. I could plant pepper and it'd be really ready to grow, too. Some folks can't raise pepper. But I've been raising pepper ever since. That's one of the things people missed when I left up there, 'cause they used to come around—"I come to git that gal to plant my pepper." See, I had a good hand for planting pepper.

We used to have smoked rabbit, too. They'd go out there and catch them, hide them, then cut their heads off and get that musk out of their thighs, and hang them right in there with that smokehouse meat. Yes sir.

They raised their own chickens, too, hens laying and sometimes hatching all downside the garden. We had big gardens. My grandfather and them made their own parry—we didn't have no wire fence—and put them together all around, and we'd plant butter beans there. Those butter beans would grow right up on all sides. We used to can them, and put them up in jars. We used to can tomatoes, too. And peaches—that was peach country—we had them all down the sides of our fields and the edge of the woods, and we'd get as much as we wanted and can them too.

My grandfather made his own bam-bams and he played an accordion. He used to have the kind with the knob on top. And all the men in the family played the guitar and banjos. They made their own banjos, too. My uncle, he could make good things. He made for white people and all. He was real tall and could he pick a guitar! Made the best banjos, too. They also made their own baskets—cotton baskets to pick cotton in—and things like that. Made their own ax handles; Pa used to make his own grinding rock out of hickory.

15

Those who farmed, some of them were sharecroppers but others were mostly renters. Instead of having to sharecrop with a man they rented the grounds that they used and renters always made something. You see, a sharecropper don't ever have nothing. Before you know it, the man done took it all. But a renter always have something, and then he go to work when he want to go to work. He ain't got to go to work on the man's time. If he didn't make it, he didn't get it. He paid for the use of the ground, had his own mule, and he had to make enough because he had to feed that mule. And besides their mules they had their own hogs, cows, and things like that. And that way you get a chance to sell your own produce—like eggs. Momma used to go to town every Wednesday and Saturday to sell eggs. Those were the days to go to town and sell eggs and brooms. People bought lots of brooms because in those days we swept the yard, not rake it. You sold brooms for ten cents apiece and sometimes you came home with decent money. Or else you swapped them for things that you needed. I know sometimes Momma would swap them for cloth out the store. So in that way, a person got a mind to make it and not to beg, didn't have to be defeated in every respect. It would be tough and they wouldn't go to the top, but they could make a way. If they try, they could do it. That's why they say when you're down you rise by trying to do something. Try to make a living, that's what they said. Even if they had to sell fish sometimes they'd do it. Catch them in the rivers and creeks and sell them. But a lot of people just don't try to make it, you know.

On these farms the white owners used to tell the people there, say, "Go back in the pastures and git the cows." Cows got calves out there, and many of them calves would go to the wrong cows and all that and it was just ruining them. Snakes were nursing the cows and all that; the cows needed tending to. And the white people would tell you to go out there and git the cow and put the cow to your house, you know, and whatever milk the cow gave, that would be your milk. And a lot of them colored folks wouldn't do it 'cause they thought the white people were playing a trick on them. Now, you see, that's silly. That's really silly. 'Cause sometimes Momma and them would have three cows round the yard. They never did have to go find no cow; just go out there and git her. Because see now, that cow is coming to you every evening. She's coming because she knows somebody gon tend to her and feed her. Now see, that's our milk, and what we didn't drink we could sell. Then here come some of them same people who say they didn't want no cow, coming to buy or ask you to give them some milk. A bucket in their hands, too! Instead of their going out there and git them a cow. That just show you that everybody ain't going to try—my grandfather often talked like that—that everybody don't care the same. And they think they're saying something big, like "If he want his cow milked let him milk it hisself. I ain't milking his cow." But it would be just like their cow if they got it in their yard.

Sometimes it was hogs. You take that old sow out there and put her in your pen and tend to her. Sometimes they may want water, sometimes they may not want anything. They'd have them young pigs down in the woods, and ain't no telling what'll happen. You go git them and have them fed. A lot of people started out like that, and after a while had plenty hogs of their own. Had their own meat, without any buying. It's just a little trouble they took to do a little something. But others! "Who? Huh, he better git his own hog. I ain't studying him. I ain't feeding no hog." That's just mess. It's just a mistake we make. We miss the boat too, 'cause we got to go buy something to eat or catch our hand stealing somebody's meat out of their crib. So anyhow, it just goes to show you that some folks will try and some won't.

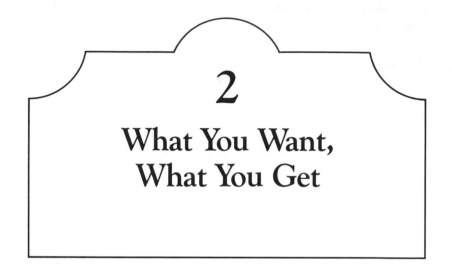

# 2

# What You Want, What You Get

WHEN I WAS a child we moved from place to place all the time. We stayed for a while at Bronwood and that's where I first went to school. I went to Hickory Level School there. That was Hickory Level Church too. This was in a place where the hickory trees were level, and they called it Hickory Level. We used to have school and church in the same building. When we moved down to Dawson I went to school there at a place called Mountain Grove. They used to name churches according to where they sit in those days, and that was a church sitting up on a high hill. I went to school in Dawson until I were about eleven years old; I wasn't twelve.

Hickory Level was three miles from where we used to live in Bronwood, but Mountain Grove was only about a mile from our house in Dawson. I used to run it, too, to school and from school, 'cause I didn't like them chillun. The chillun were bad! They'd fight all the time and I never did like fighting and I would run ahead of them each way. When I came out of the schoolhouse I would just go right on, 'cause I didn't want to be bothered with them. They used to make fun of me 'cause they saw I was fat to them, with bowlegs. Say, "Look at Liz: look like father hooks legs. Yeah, look like father hooks." And I'd just run. But anyway, I stayed away from them.

In Dawson my momma had a cousin; her name was Elizabeth. She had her arm cut off when she was a little girl down in Milan but she was a big solid woman then, and from childhood had learned to handle that arm. You know how they learn to handle that part that never been broke. I was scared of her. I ain't too good with it now—a nub without anything on it. Ooh, great God! I was scared of it. Elizabeth knew that and her husband knew that. So one day Elizabeth heard about me running from them chillun so they wouldn't pick at me. And so she says, she told Momma she was going to walk home with me one day and she wasn't going to let me run. I didn't like that. But one day she did go home with me and she say, "I'm going home with you today and I want to see that you don't run from these children. If they want to fight you, you better fight them." I got so scared. She say, "If you don't, I'm going to whip you." Well I knew good and well how she going to have to whip me. She had to hold me down with that nub, you see, and I didn't want that nub on me. Ooh, Lord! You ought to know the condition I was in that day.

I looked at Elizabeth and I looked at the chillun and I was hoping they wouldn't bother me 'cause I didn't want to be messed with that nub. And so we went on. Till after a while the chillun started picking. Little old Callie, she started to picking at me: "I can beat you Liz." She talked real heavy and was about a year and something older than me. "I can beat you if you don't run from me. You'd better, 'cause I'll sure whip you Liz." I didn't say nothing to her. So we got on the bridge there and Elizabeth leaned up against that railing. I know now that she wasn't going to let her whip me, but I didn't then and I knew I didn't like all that fighting. So I looked at Callie; Callie kept on. Callie clowned on. She carried on like a woman. You know they used to have a habit in those days what they call shaking your collar. And so she started up there to shake my collar. And I knew her brother. I wasn't worried about her; her brother was the bad thing. Terrible bad. And I never played with boys much on account of them slingshots they had and other things. They were just a little too rough for me. When I did play with little boys I played with them 'cause I was alone and didn't have no sisters or brothers. And I'm telling myself, I reckon I'll just sit. But I didn't want to worry Elizabeth and I didn't want Callie shaking my collar and so I just grabbed her. I grabbed Callie. I don't know how I done it but I threw her overboard, over that bannister. It was so quick it was beautiful.

The creek was a heavy creek called Valley Creek, and right at the bridge it had a big curve in it and that water was hustling. That water be going, you hear! Oh boy. But when I throwed her in there, then I got scared. I wouldn't say nothing to nobody else and I was gone. I was gone home, you hear! Making it to Momma. Elizabeth wasn't gon whip me. I threw Callie over that board and Elizabeth ain't had time to fool with me again. I looked back, and the boys around that bridge were pulling off their coats and diving in that water. And I run over that hill and told Momma Callie grabbed me to whip me and I pushed her in the water.

Later on here they come; a lot of them wet but they had got Callie out of that water. I told Momma, say, I run from Callie's brothers and them 'cause I didn't want them to catch me. And so Momma didn't say nothing. The crowd came on up and she found out how it was. Wasn't nothing she could whip me about. Then Elizabeth say, "I meant for them to fight. But Liz grabbed her so quick and throwed her in that water so quick, left everybody wondering." Was that peaceable Liz? Such a peaceable girl! (Some of them same chillun used to eat up my food.) Everybody was there. And Callie was wet. Her mother and different ones came down when they heard about it. And so when Mrs. Winters—that was Callie's momma—and them came down there, Momma say, "Don't feel sick. She got enough about hitting out in that water." Mrs. Winter say, "Uh, uh. I'm going to whip Callie." You could hear her, too. I mean, when she tied that gal, she whipped that gal, you hear me! She give that girl a beating. She said she didn't know this was going on, and none of them knew this was going on, see, 'cause I was outrunning them chillun every day. And so from that day on, that settled it. I didn't have no trouble like that any more.

I stammered so bad in those days, I couldn't talk, I stammer now—whether people notice it or not—but I stammer. I learned how to bring out words as good as I do now after I was around seventeen years old. I used to stammer so until you could almost walk across the street before I could get a word out. I'd just hit myself and knock, and stomp, trying to bring out the words, and so that's why I never got no whipping in school. I was always working so hard to talk, I never had time for trouble; never have got a beating in school, no kind. But I was afraid of it. I was afraid that I was going to git a whipping, 'cause in those days they had lodges used to meet in a corner of the school, and right in the church pulpit they had a big bundle of switches—long black switches. Either them gallberry switches or some other kind; them boys would go and cut them switches and put them up there. And I seen them chillun get a whipping—not bloody whippings, just striking them across the shoulder and they be just flinching and carrying on.

The first school I went to, that's Hickory Level, that woman there, she'd beat the blood out of you. But my aunt and momma went down there one day and got her. Oh yeah. They went down there and got her behind that junk. She whipped Lula one day, and I just kept looking up there 'cause she wouldn't stop beating Lula on the legs, you know, and her hands. And finally I broke from the school running. She put the boys behind me to catch me because she knew I was going home to tell it. I got out of there and hit that railroad—was a railroad up there—and I run, and when I looked back and seen them chillun coming behind me it looked like they were going to catch me, you know, and I knew I was going to get a whipping if I had to go back there. And I went to the deacon of the church—I didn't know he was a deacon then but I learned it since—who had a big farmhouse and a wagon shed with buggies and wagons in it. I dodged them children under there. I went and I dodged them and they went but they couldn't find me. I went way on all the way around them fields until I come to where I knew where I was, then I went home through the woods and fields. When I got there Momma and them were working in the field hoeing cotton. They seen me coming and didn't know what in the world had happened. So I told them. I told them that the teacher was up there beating the blood out of Lula.

They didn't say a word. They throwed their hoes down and started for the school in them long dresses, just like they were—barefooted as a gopher—and they came right on through 'cause they knew how to get there quicker than I ran, and they made them chillun turn around and get right behind them. Made them run every step of the way back. They were angry. The chillun run in there; they say, "Lizabeth done got home; Lizabeth done got home. Liz's momma and them are coming." It was Annie and Momma, you see; Annie was raising Lula since Lula's momma, Aunt Chery, had died. So anyhow, we got there and they called out that teacher. She was a red woman, and Momma called her all kinds of funny things while she just standing up there looking at them. And she thought she was so cute! I thought she was too. When I started to school there I went to her. I wanted her to be my teacher, 'cause she was so pretty. But she was the meanest thing you ever seen. She would beat you to death. And so they expelled her from school. Yeah, she got expelled from school, she was so mean. Her name was Miss Edna. I thought she was the cutest but they didn't allow you to beat blood out of the chillun; they didn't allow that at all. And Lula wasn't saying ne'er a word, just standing there looking down mumbling, "Yes'm, yes'm, yes'm," and that teacher was just tearing her up.

When I first went there to school, I'd been learning my ABCs from a boy named Billy Kitchen and Lula, and I knowed about half of that book just by heart. Whenever they'd teach me, they'd point to the letters with a pencil or a stick or something like that and that's the only way I'd been taught. So the first day of school—I remember the teacher had one of her lady friends visiting her—I went to the teacher and I couldn't talk 'cause I was stammering so bad. She say, "Come here," and I went to the door where she was. She say, "Git down there," and I got down on one knee side of her. She pointed in the book with her finger and said, "What is this?" I say "A finger," and them folks laughed. They laughed until they liked to cry; I never will forget that. I didn't know what in the world they were laughing about.

She put her hand up there, she say, "What is that?" I'd never been taught that way with no finger, never in my life, so I said it was a finger, that what it was. And so then they laughed so until I went and got Lula. When Lula got there she asked what I had done and the teacher say, "She don't know her *A* from her finger. She called an *A* a finger." Lula said, "Uh, uh." She say, "Lizabeth know her ABCs." I say, "She put a finger up, and that was a finger." The head teacher then say, "Teacher her with a pencil; that's what I teach with." See, Miss Edna was assistant teacher and she laughed us down that first day. Then later on she beat the blood out of Lula.

Before she beat Lula there was a boy there named Charlie Kitchen—he come to be my cousin in a way when his son married into our family—he used to bring the switches in for the teacher and was on her good side. He was a good-sized boy, and nice-looking, and she flirted at him. I didn't know what that meant in those days, but he knew it and then he told it. She got at him about that and wanted to beat him. He told her, "I'll take this baseball bat and kill you." He had a baseball bat. But they squashed it at that, and a little later on she beat the blood out of Lula, and then, see, she had to go.

After Lula got grown she married to Pat Taylor. He was one of the boys I used to run from so fast though he never really was aiming at me. Oh, that was a bad boy. I ain't never seen him bother no girls, but them boys, you see, they'd fight, and that Pat would just turn them over. He used to butt, too; that boy was a butter. Ooh, that Pat was something else. But Lula married him, and they had fourteen children. I know Pat's dead now. I don't know whether Lula is alive or not. Last I heard she were in Wildwood, Florida. I don't know if she's still down there or not.

Outside of school we had chores in those days. Not them little things kids do now, pickin' up this and that. We had to help out. We used to have to scour our floors, not scrub like the people call it now, and not mop. We scoured our floors with a scouring mop. We used shucks and wood to make that mop. We'd make a handle like a hoe handle, then soak the shucks and work the soft side into the handle and leave the rough side to work with. When you scrub that floor, you make that floor so clean! And the floors used to be made out of them old wide planks. And we had wooden shutter windows; we scoured them, too. And that's the difference in sickness today. We scrubbed our chairs and everything on Friday or Saturday mornings, make them all clean. We scalded every year once a year. We'd take everything out of the house and scald it. Pour hot water all over the place, and scoured it. But now they cover up the disease with all kinds of spray and paint and stuff. You lay down, and at night you're inhaling it right on if you don't keep your household clean. That's why so much sickness. We scalded all that, and killed all the germs. And we had underhouses in those days, too. We had a house up on blocks so you could get up under there and clean.

Then again we helped with raising money if we could. When I was a little girl about eight years old in Dawson, we used to pick huckleberries. Sometimes we'd pick them for canning, sometimes for cooking. Not far from the farm where I stayed there was a little skin of woods and we had to pass through there to get to our friend's house. On the way going there, on one side they had a hogpen, and on the righthand side of that pass in the warm weather, we'd play there with our dolls and things. We used to have old rag dolls made out of grass and old rags. Well, we'd play there on Sundays after Sunday school when we weren't allowed to sit around with the grownups. Now and then you can find some pine in that part of the country, and there were some pine trees on the righthand side there and we had these pines as our riding horses. We had a flying jinny and all our other stuff down there to play with, and some Sundays it would be the same chillun, other Sundays it would be strange chillun, but that was our playground. We had beds made up of leaves and straw and we made as though we had rooms in a house and played mom and dad, and cooking, and all like that. There was a little weed down there called coffee weed, grew a bean on it. We used to take those beans and put them in empty sardine cans and pretend we were cooking. We used to have a grand time there.

One day Momma and them were picking huckleberries to sell,

and Miss Susan—a white woman Momma was working for—told Momma if she picked up there in the woods to bring her some because she wanted to can. There were plenty of huckleberries and shankie pins in that side of the woods. Shankie pins was a fuzzy-looking kind of nut we used to crack and eat right off the bush when it was dry; tastes something like peanuts, and look most like a cockleburr. Well anyway, snakes love these things. So they told us to pick the berries, and Momma knew where some huckleberries were back up behind the hogpen. Up the little hill from the hogpen was a place where the men used to gamble— they never gambled in front of the children—and it was very, very clean. There was a huge log which must've been cut down years before, and they'd make a fire there and sit down on the log and that was their gambling ground. Just above it was a bunch of huckleberries—they grow tall in that country and I liked to pull them down to me, and sometimes eat a bunch while I was picking.

So we were picking berries and I think it was on a Monday, because Momma was going to buy me a dress for church that next Sunday when Miss Susan paid her for the huckleberries we picked. Momma had a big bucket and I had a little one. We picked and we picked, and after a while we heard something. Momma didn't know anything about snakes such as their keeping noise. This thing said "Thupp!" then it kept a noise. Momma said, "I hear some kind of big bug." I was standing up stretching for some berries, holding my bucket on my arm, leaning over picking berries. This thing just kept up this noise down there and I couldn't see anything because the bushes were so thick. But the Lord knows when to come in there. This thing got to singing so loud, Momma said, "Let me see what kind of bug that is." When she said that, the bush I was pulling on was the same bush some of this thing was hanging on, and see, it was a rattle-snake and he was setting for my face. I didn't move. If I had moved my face that would've been it, because as Momma said "Let me see what kind of a bug that is" she pulled the bush, and he struck right past me. I screamed, "Oh Lordy, Momma, there he is!" Momma jumped back. She said "Whoo!" She hollered. But I looked at that thing. When he hit past me I was looking right into his mouth, and I saw inside of him, and I looked at him stretched out, and Momma said, "Come on, let's go." So we left, and picked our berries at another spot, until Momma looked at me and saw that I was scared, and she said, "Let's go home."

When we got to the house, Momma said there was some kind of old big bug out there in the bushes and it scared us. "It scared Bess," she said. I said, "Momma, that wasn't no bug, that was a rattlesnake." Momma said, "No, it was a bug." She had only seen him when he was a lump keeping that noise, and then he jumped, and that's what made Momma think it was a bug. When she realized it was a snake she said, "Oh Lord, my child almost got killed!" She put me across her lap. "That snake, that rattlesnake. Oh Goodness!" I was eight years old and never will forget it.

I'll never forget Andrew Slade neither. He was a man who stayed around there, and the Robinson show—that old minstrel show my uncle ran off with—was paying people to get snakes for them. All the snakes you caught you sent to them and they would pay you. This man Andrew, he was a snake-catcher but he was on the other side of town gathering snakes. Momma went to some white folks' house and they called Miss Susan—they had funny telephones in the box in those days—and told her what had happened. She said she would send Andrew. But my grandfather and them knew about snakes, and he said, "Wherever he was then he's there now." But Momma was too scared to go and show them the spot. They went with their ax handles and hoes and things, but didn't see anything. They came back after they couldn't find him and said to Momma, "You come and show us." So we went down there. Momma went up on the hill and I went just far enough to see the stump and I said, "You see that stump there, Pa. He was over there." Pa took a lot of knots and chunked them over there and the snake said "Vrrrrr!" every time Pa chunked those knots. They were right; they knew rattlesnakes just that well. But they decided not to kill it because Miss Susan was sending Andrew over.

Miss Susan sent that man out there, and he had him a horse and buggy. That man came on down through those woods, to that same pass where we played every Sunday. He had some kind of funny stuff on him but he was a snake charmer. He blew that thing in his mouth and the snakes came right around him as though he had called chickens that were his pets. They came up and wrapped themselves around him, all around his neck, and he would just grab one, jerk its mouth open and put his hand in there and pull out that bag. It was miserable for me. So miserable for me to see all those snakes, and that thing inside the snake's mouth when he hit past me, and all, that Momma had to send me away from that place to rest afterwards. But anyway, Andrew caught them snakes that day, and then he went over to the log where the men used to gamble and he got fifteen snakes out of that log. He got about forty-eight out of the woods.

This was on a Monday. Mr. Coop Fish had stayed there all night the night before, because they'd been gambling and wouldn't give him any more money when he lost, so he layed down on the log and went to sleep and stayed there all night. He got up the next morning and went on to the lot to go to work. When they told Coop about the snakes, he fainted. They got fifteen snakes out of that log; they came crawling out to the man. No more gambling there, brother! No more gambling there. Andrew's buggy had sections separated by screen wire and when you looked, he had one kind of snake in this section, another kind in that section, and they were winding up all over one another—it was a sight. From that day to this I don't pick huckleberries for nobody unless I see some on the side of the road and I can see all under that bush that there ain't nothing around it.

People showed us children respect back in my childhood days, too. Just like the men not gambling out in the open where everybody passing could see them, folks back then didn't want nobody's children to see them doing wrong, and so they would hide from you. Nowadays folks don't care; they let the children see them drunk or they cuss before the children, and everything else. But in those days they didn't do it. Now there was this woman there who had lived sometime in town, I think, and used to have the stuff they call cocaine. She would wear high-top shoes and her name was Bessie. Bessie Daniels. And so the folks next from us, their well went dry, and they had to tote water from our well.

So Edna was coming at some water over there one day and she seen Miss Bessie. Miss Bessie was drunk, and was trying to hide from the chillun to get to her house. Her hair was loose all over her head, her high-heel shoes were loose, her eyes all stretched wide open, and Edna called us and showed her to us. I looked, and seen her, and that was the worst sight I'd ever seen in my life. I had to run from her. I'd never seen my grandfather's house without whiskey, but nobody ever got drunk, or acted like they were drunk. But when I went to the stoop by our chimney I could see her and how she was trying to dodge us and hide her eyes and everything under there. I thought that was the worse-looking woman I'd ever seen in my life and I said I never wanted nobody calling me Miss ol' Bessie. I meant it to my heart, 'cause I was so mad at that woman. And see what God did for me!

A man told me this in Baltimore one day. He said, "You didn't want to be called Miss old bad Bessie, but God blessed you: you Miss good Bessie. See, you Bessie right on, let you know that He take care of that Bessie too. He take care of that Bessie just like He take care of you." See, wasn't nothing the matter with it but I truly didn't want to be called no Bessie. And God fixed it. Said, "I'm gon show you; you're gonna go through a theme of Bessie. That my woman too." That Bessie was his woman, wasn't mine. But I didn't like her because she was drunk. She was trying to hide from us and we were trying to find her and see her. But nowadays you don't have to try to find them; you got to try to run from them. You see old drunk women in the streets, you tell the chillun, "Go in the house, go in the house. Move out of the way." 'Cause she coming and she ain't worried about you now.

But see, in those days people were different. A man didn't gamble around where his children were at, not in his house nor around his wife or nothing. They'd go in an old shack house or back in the woods or somewhere to gamble. But they have no respect now, none at all. They'd have their children there holding the light for them if they have to have one. It's different these days and it's pitiful. I just stay scared all the time and go ahead on about my business. Lord, it's a great change since I been born, yes sir. And they say, "Them the old days." In some instances I'd rather have them. You got more respect. I'd rather have them in some instances, not for the welfare of living, but for the love and care of one another. 'Cause since people done got so much freedom they don't care about nothing more. Not like they used to. People don't wait on one another like they used to. In those days, people got sick and others would wait on you and help you. But now you can't hardly find that. Sometimes now people come to your house when you're sick and they ask, I'm telling you, they ask is anything you want them to do for you. That's right. Now them that come in and say I want to straighten this for you or I'm going to fix some soup for you or either I'm gonna make up your bed or rake the yard, now that I can understand. But them others that have to ask, you know they don't care none about you really, and probably don't care none about theirself.

But that's why I'm called Bessie. 'Cause I slurred the woman I had no business to slur.

And there was a woman stayed there named Mrs. Laura Richardson. They were farmers too and she had a little fat boy named Joe. Joseph Richardson. And Joe would chunk rocks at me. I didn't have anybody to play with and I'd have to go down behind the house to play, and every time I'd go down there I had to dodge hickory nuts and rocks. I'd dodge till I got to him, then I'd whip him. I'd beat him 'cause he never would fight. He'd be saying, "Oh Liz, oh Liz," and I'd be beating him. And it got so that I hated him and I said I didn't want nobody in my house called Joe. Nobody. Never. No Joe of mine. And look what I got! My baby son is Joseph, his older son is Joseph, and his baby son has another Joseph. I got little Joes and big Joe but I didn't want it. Just goes to show you never know how it differs, what you want and what you're going to get.

# 3

# Frolics and a Picture

AS A CHILD people always used to say I was very musical, and most of my life has been taken up with music. My mother used to play the autoharp—they were different then from what they are now, the way you used to tune them up—and up in Dawson she bought me an accordion. Later on I bought me a guitar. I can fram a guitar now but I can't pick it. In those days we didn't have parties—so-called parties—we had frolics. And then we'd have different musicians with accordions and banjos and we'd have a big time. But I was scared of a banjo—big-belly man with a long neck. That's what they used to say he was—big-belly man with a long neck. When I was a little girl I didn't like getting around them things. I wasn't scared of the fiddle but they pitied him. Say the fiddle is like a little baby and they didn't want anybody meddling with him. And when he called his neighbors, poor li'l thing, he was just crying. But the banjo is different now; they so big and round. They're made up prettier, all fancy. Poppa and them used to make them, great big African banjo we called it. They made them out of wood, and I don't know where they got the string from, but they made them and then they put rattlesnake rattles in them. After they caught the rattlesnakes they'd make belts out of the skins, and they'd take the rattles and let them dry out, then put them into the guitar or the banjo, either one. It gives a great tone. And you can do it now; it's the same thing. It makes a great tone. My grandfather made his own bam-bam, too, and chairs, and such. They made lots of things for themselves in those days.

Music has always been a big part in my life, but in those early days we had the church too, and I was brought up in a church, liked to go to church and go to meetings and everything, but I didn't like no preacher. You see, in those days when I was coming up little, if you were the pastor of a church, widows and such who had chillun getting unruly would tell you about it, and you were supposed to help make those chillun mind. I've known Reverend Perry to come out of church and bring that buggy whip with him to see about chillun getting sassy with their momma. Yes sir. Mary Jane was sassy. She was growing up right with me, same time, and old Mary Jane used to get behind the bed—they had a big old house—and he would whip her out from under that bed. He never would hurt her bad, just enough to make her mind, but that made me mad and I didn't want no preacher in my house. None at all. I understand now what I didn't understand then. If you ain't got no husband and you're a widow, then the preacher is supposed to come and help. His wife, too, is supposed to come and help get those chillun straight in that house. Help that woman if she needed help. But all I saw was there's that preacher; yon he walk. He gonna beat them chillun. Course he was doing right but I didn't want that. And God said, "I'm going to fix you. I'm going to let you birth one." See, my older son is a pastor. I'm telling you, you don't know what you're going to do!

In those days after you got a whipping or something like that we used to beat our mommas, stomp on them, and bury them— only they didn't know it. We'd get a long stick with knots in it or some piece of wood or something and name it her. And we'd go down in the back and beat the devil out of it. Beat Grandma; call her all kinds of stuff. We'd just tear them up, then go back home looking nice. You better go in there looking nice. That's right. But we felt good, just like Pa and them would when they sung songs. We done beat you and we really felt good. They never knew that we tore them up, or that would've been a whipping.

But kids don't do that now; they cuss their real momma and like that. There's a boy in Brunswick that was just sentenced the other day. He got eighty years. He used to cuss his momma like a dog. And I woke up the other morning thinking about it, and I was so worried thinking about his spending all his young days under the gun, all those many years, and it really got on me and a thought come to me: the disobedient child shall never taste grace. I say, "God, I can't handle your business." See, that boy used to cuss his momma out, chunk things in the house and tear things up. But when I heard the sentence, I didn't think about that. Yet, I don't care what you do, you can't get by the Lord. I didn't want this and I didn't want that but I got it all. Got every bit of it.

I didn't have to be baptized when I was little because my grandfather, my mother, and all of them didn't believe in baptizing children since children don't know anything about that water you pour on them. Ain't no need in sprinkling around like that and they just didn't do it. I wasn't baptized as a child but I had to go to church, Sunday school and church. I got converted when I was seventeen years old and that's when I got baptized. That was in Fitzgerald. You had to do something in those days—the crew that I came along with—to prove yourself. You couldn't just walk up to be baptized, and I'm glad of it. People prayed and cried over us and we had to pray too. Some of us came through and some didn't, quite naturally, but I often think of the vision I had when I was praying there.

A man came up to me in this vision and he was real tall. I was standing and he came up to me with a little book or something in his hand. He took this book and he brought some cards out of it—look like address cards—and the first one had a church on it. The next card he brought out had a church on it and the next one had a church on it. He brought out three cards, all with churches. Two of the churches had steeples and the other church didn't have a steeple. He passed that card to me—the one that didn't have a steeple. I didn't know what it meant for a long time, then it came to me and I knew. The two big churches had steeples, yet the little church without a steeple, basically that was great. The writing beneath the church on that card said, "Holy." There was no writing on the other cards at all. So I figured that thing out and I joined the church then.

The day I got baptized—baptized in a millpond—in this little pond there was a suck-hole. A lot of folks teased us about that thing. They had a staff stuck down there for the preacher and you could feel that water pulling at you. They had to hold you; we were that close to the suck-hole. A man and his roadcart had gone down in that thing once, 'cause his ox wanted water and when a cow wants water he ain't joking; he's going to get it. And this ox stood his feet in the pond and ducked his head for the water. The man tried to pull the ox back and lost his own life. No man can pull an ox back. We used to take great big logs and shove them over there, and now a log would usually stay afloat but there that log would turn on end and it'd go down. That was a suck-hole!

The funniest thing: when we got baptized, there was a lady there that day named Mary. Mary came out there and they just had to hold her. She was hollering and oh she was hollering. She had a wicked husband named George and he was standing right there. George said—he got to mocking Mary—"Lord I'm so glad I didn't go down in that suck-hole! Lord I'm so glad I didn't go down in that suck-hole." And when Mary turned around like she wanted to go back, he said she was looking back as if to say, "I'm sure glad I didn't go down in that suck-hole. Thank you Jesus!" We had fun that day. And during the fellowship that night I was so tickled because George had teased her so bad Mary was angry. She was fit to be tied. And George was still teasing her. Lord, we had some fun in those days!

But the Lord blessed me. I never was all that good until I came to be born again; I wasn't born again when I got baptized, I was just converted, but I thank God for it. Later on I was born again when I was in Okeechobee, Florida, where I stayed a long time. To be born again you have to be baptized again and I was baptized again—quite naturally. When you're born again you join a membership but you are the church. That's where I'm at now. We join this membership and we go to the same building, but when Jesus says I'm coming to the church, He ain't coming to that thing out there; He's coming to you. You are the church. I am the church. Sometimes folks ask me, "What church do you belong to?" and I say, "I belong to myself." I am the church. If your body is the temple for the Holy Ghost to dwell in and if you believe, you might as well believe in that church.

My grandfather used to teach us all that, too. You never knew where some people had the Holy Ghost sometimes because so many of them had it and didn't even know. They used to sing the song about "The comforter has come/The Holy Ghost in heaven/ That Father's promise given," and that's true. They had it. But they didn't know how to name it and they went under the name of some other church. But in themselves they were saved. I was brought up in that way. And they'd sing that song, "The comforter has come," and that comforter wasn't nothing but the Holy Ghost itself and that's it. And so anyhow, they had it. The true light was coming. By them not having much understanding in reading, the part that God handed down to them, they sure used it. All those songs that were handed down to them without notes, without any education—you think about it! That's why I like to keep it up. I keep up the slave songs that they learned in church, and the play songs too, and the stories, the riddles and things.

Yet people had fun times those days in Dawson too. Momma and them gave frolics or went to somebody else's frolic regularly. They wouldn't go to places that were too rough or where there wouldn't be any respect for the house, with people using all kinds of language. You know, it's natural, when you come in people's house you're supposed to respect them in their own house if they got any respect there. But if there aint' none there, you don't care. And especially the places they called outlaw places, Momma and them wouldn't go there. My grandfather and them used to make their own whiskey out of corn, then let it stand for three, four, or five years before they drink it, and I ain't never seen any one of them drunk. Never seen any one of them act like they were drunk, although I have seen other people drunk and I didn't like it. But when Momma and them gave frolics at our house they didn't allow any cutting up and acting. And when we got older and people weren't giving frolics but were having candy-pullings and egg-crackings and parties like that, they still called themselves respectable, and never had any flirting or nothing like that.

There were many games they played back then. At an egg-cracking there would be tubs of boiled eggs, and each person would buy about three, and then see how many eggs they could crack with their own. You'd knock your egg against somebody else's—the sharp ends—and if my egg cracked your egg then I won it. That way a person could start with just a few eggs and leave with many. These were parties to help out somebody who was sick, or the church, and you'd pay for all your eggs that got cracked—sometimes a quarter for every one—and all the money was turned over to the cause, whatever it was. In those days a quarter was big money. If you had a boiled rotten egg it would crack them all and you'd go home with a big bucket of eggs. It was fun and I liked those parties.

I never did like the apple game but I liked to watch them doing it. Apple-biting. They'd put apples in a tub of water and every-body dipped down there to pick up the apples with their mouths. I didn't ever like that because I didn't want to put my mouth in that water. But string-chewing I used to like. That's where you put an apple in the middle of a string, and a person stands on either end, then try to see which one could chew through to the apple first. And sometimes you could tie a banana, or anything, onto the string. Whoever got there first, then that's his fruit. But you're not supposed to put your hands on the string. That used mostly to be a kids' game.

Another game we used to play was "drawing peanuts." That's when you brought one or five or any number of packets of pea-nuts and put them out on the table. Then you start drawing and everybody takes one until the last one. Whoever gets the last one paid for the whole thing. That was fun.

At frolics, they used to do a set-dance but they used to stay on their feet, no kicking and pulling all over the shoulder and that kind of stuff. They had different pretty turns and marches. There would be a man in front who called the sets and usually there were sixteen, or half that number, in the ring. When they came into the frolic to dance, you could tell who was the head and who was the feet by the way they were dressed. The head woman wore the prettiest apron: not a cook's apron, but an apron with a big belt in it, with a big bow at the back, and pockets embroidered and fixed with real beauty. Sometimes they'd have a pretty bow in her hair. And the head man, he wore a long scarf around his neck that was either white or pink. They'd wear that until somebody beat them dancing, then they'd have to give it to the better ones.

But a set's a dancing thing and when they called them they'd get all sixteen of them. They'd all get together and hold hands in a pure ring, then they'd say "Balance A," and you'd do that; then "Balance B," and you'd do that too. Then "Circle to the right," that meant walk to your right; "Circle to the left"; then "Halfway back," and you come right back to where you started. Then it's opened up to the first lady. "First lady dances to the right," and she got to dance out in the ring by herself. She dances up to her partner and she turns him, then she dances to the next lady's partner and she turns him, comes back to her partner and turns her own. She dances on all around until she gets to the last man, but she has to turn her partner again after every one. Then the second woman goes around, then the third and they do the same thing. The women always went first. Then the call would be for "The first old man," and he'd do the same thing—dance to the right, then dance to his partner, and then the other partners. Then all the other men would follow. After the second round they'd promenade, and after the promenade they'd drop back.

They had drop back number one—you'd drop back and get that one partner—then drop back number two, and you kept on dropping back until you got to number four or your own partner, then you corner swing. Then they'd call "Women in the middle and men all around"; the women then stood back to back in the middle as the men went around. Then as the men went around they stopped and danced with the one opposite their partner. Then you "Swing your own and get her back"—oh, that's the prettiest thing! Now that's really dancing! And that way, they found out how good you could dance, 'cause a good set-caller would make you do it. You had to learn how to call a set. We had a man named Mr. Noble Harris; that man sounded like Marvin Jackson—Marvin Jackson was a preacher—and he could do it. The music would be going and he'd be just doing it. And then they'd have him to do what they called "Shoo fly." I like that. "Shoo fly, li'l woman, shoo fly." You're swinging now. You ain't stopping to dance with anybody. And the man, he comes out and he does the same thing. You'd be going and you put what movement you got into it. You don't just walk; you got to have movement with the music. They'd have guitars, harps, anything that people could play together in one corner, and that music would be together. I used to beat the guitar with the straws when I grew and was going to frolics myself. You'd take the broom straw and beat the guitar strings, and that'd make the guitar sound good. Oh, do it!

Then you'd know who was the best dancer by the way he danced and the steps he cut. You could cut any way you wanted to but that best dancer, he got it. And when you came in there and beat the best dancer, that ring got back and let them dance together for a little while to be sure. You test dance. Women the same thing. They used to have a dance they called "The Sinking Titanic," where you danced that sinking. Oh Lord, those folks could do that dance! You go straight backwards and down to the floor with your hips, and go on down. Course they wore long dresses in those days to sink that Titanic. You couldn't do it now; these girls ain't got no clothes. They had it so you could see who could sink it the best, or who could "Ball the Jack," but I let them go on. It's alright, just go on and do it; don't worry about it. But that was the best dancing.

Then they'd go to the table, which was all set, because folks had those frolics to build churches, help choirs, help the preacher, or somebody sick, or anything like that, and all that was taken up there went for whatever the purpose was.

When I was a little girl and they had frolics at our house, when the time came for bed, I'd have to go. But I'd listen and hear them sets called, and would get the children together a day or two from that and call the sets. The children would do that dance. So I used to stand right behind them, looking at them, all the time.

All the children can't get around alike, you know. We expect the same energy in all children, but some of them are stiff and everybody ain't cut out for a dancer. So Pa would show us how to do it. Then with the clapping of hands, he'd teach us the different claps—baritone, base, and tenor—and show us how to do it. And he made those little things that are called limberjacks out of shingle, and showed us how to make them dance the buck dance.

Buck dancing was the real thing in those days. There were twenty-one different breaks in the buck. So they'd teach the children how to do it, those of us that could do it. But me, I never could do the buck dance. I had a cousin and she could do it. But I never got it to work right: too parrot-toed and too bowlegged. Buck dancing is a pretty dance and it tells a whole lot of stories back in there. Every break has its own name, and those people used to dance them, too, from dressing up to see your gal, to stepping out, and getting out of tough. But that was for their own fun: that wasn't talking to massa.

Sometimes when the shows came to town, Momma and them would carry their little wood-bottom stoves and things over there, and sell fish and stuff on the main street, and Aunt Margaret used to keep all the peoples' chillun while they were out selling. And when the big show came, we used to go out and look at the parade—the elephants and different animals and clowns and all sorts of things—and my poppa used to sit up on the elephants and ride them. He and the other men who went early in the morning to help the circus unload could ride the animals into town and then their families could get into the show free. It usually rained when the show came to town, too, because they'd bring the thing called a mermaid, and whenever they brung that you could look for rain. There was something about it: if she cried it rained.

Anyhow, one time they were there, and it was raining, and the street was muddy and they had a lion there they called the biggest in the world. He was in a cage all by himself. There was a man named Mr. Carter who had mixed children—some were dark, some were red—and Son, his second child, went into the fairgrounds where the circus was set up, and he stood near the cages where the lions were, and didn't that thing roar! The glasses in Aunt Margaret's house half a mile away jarred together. It was trouble in Dawson that day! People were scared; they were running, some were screaming and falling over one another, and a lot of them who knew Aunt Margaret were coming to her house because their chillun were there. They were piling in the house on top of one another and that lion kept roaring. The show people wanted to know what was the cause of this, and they decided to search everybody who was in there. They shut the doors and began searching people. And finally they found Son, the same boy we used to play with. They got everybody back, and when they brought Son near that cage those lions started up again, and they found what it was. First, Son had just shaved and had cut some bumps on his face. The next thing was, he had a very peculiar odor, he sure did, he and his sister and all the red ones in the family. It was an odor like fresh beef. Every one of them had that odor like fresh beef. And of course the lion had smelled him. They told him that day never to go in a show again where he was going to be around circus animals like lions and tigers and leopards.

We never had much real trouble with people coming to our house and jumping on folks as I heard talk they did other places. But growing up in a place like Dawson you had to be careful. A whole lot of times people stick their necks in places where they shouldn't be and bring things on themselves. Let's say if you were on a plantation where the white men liked colored women and you're a woman flirting, and grinning at them and giving yourself in, they'll get hot with that negro man and then try to get him out of the way so they can be with that woman. Now the black woman's got no business causing such a thing. Though sometimes they did it for that little forty or fifty cents because they never had any money. And if that white man give her ten or fifteen dollars, that was great money. Then she'd pop off and that caused trouble. Sometimes, again, the white people were just mean, hateful, and wanted to drive a colored person. But it wasn't all the time just pure meanness; they do like colored women. But if she stayed in her place and didn't mess with them, they'd leave you alone and that would save her daddy or her brother or what-not from getting into trouble. Because after you start messing with crackers they don't like you going with your own color.

There was a young colored girl up there, we called her Too-tall. She was just a tall girl but she was most beautiful, and there weren't too many tall people with pretty shapes but she had one. She was up-to-date; went to high school and everything. And those white men got around her, trying to get her off in the woods, and she wouldn't deal with that. But they kept on and finally she had to leave there. They told her she was just too good-looking for a nigger man. Her mother sent her away to keep down trouble, because if she hadn't they might've killed her. They might've found her head sawed off some day, because the wrong kind of crackers were picking at her. It was a hard place to raise daughters—especially the pretty ones. Although there were cases where white folks from some plantations would go and tell the other white owners to tell their hands to leave their people alone. In those days around Dawson there were more half-white children up there than colored ones.

Every once in a while there'd be folks the white people wouldn't mess with. My Uncle Liko was one of them. He was my grand-uncle on my stepfather's side. He had a little cafe there but he was a slicker. He'd been in a rousing show for years—ever since they first came out—then he married a little teenie woman named Millie. He was a great big old thing. Momma used to leave me at his cafe while they went shopping around in town. They'd go and get the round—anything you wanted for the year 'round like wares, clothes, and like that on credit, and put it on the farm book. You never got anything off the farm anyhow, so that's how it was.

When my uncle who had run off with the minstrel show got lynched that was in Cuthbert, Georgia. Randolph County. I was pretty small then but I remember it. Uncle Son was staying with his Uncle James—my granduncle—and Uncle James never did farm. He would always rent. He had his own mules and everything; and in those days the crackers didn't want to see the Negro have nothing. Then Uncle James gave Son a piece of ground for his part, and they were doing well until they came to find out the crackers didn't like them at all—that cracker don't like you nohow, quite naturally. The crackers did all sorts of things to them, and so they fought back—quite naturally. That was all the crackers wanted: they lied on Son and said he was flirting at one of the girls when they were somewhere swapping mules. The girl told the truth and said that Uncle Son had never said anything to her, but they told her she was just scared and lying. The girl said he never did, and she died with that same thing. But they were just mean and wanted to get at Son and this gave them an excuse. So they got behind Son.

We were at Dawson and he was coming back from the trading and they got the dogs behind him. They ran him for about two weeks. I remember the day: my cousin Lula and myself were drawing dolls in the sand in our yard. We'd lay down flat and draw one another with our fingers, and we were doing that, playing in the yard, and Son came through there. That was the last time I saw him. He picked me up and kissed me, grabbed Lula and kissed her, then he went into the kitchen, where we had an open safe, and got him a handful of food. He came out and went on across the field to where Momma and them were working. It wasn't too long after he left before the dogs came there. They came right up to the house, went around the kitchen, then took off straight across the field. By then Momma and them had already taken up Son on a mule and taken him further. Then Momma came on back home, because if she'd stayed there it would've been bad—they would've killed her too.

41

About a week or two later, the white man where we stayed came and told Momma that there was a man came through there, said he was running, going somewhere, and they had given him a bag of teacakes. And that was Son. Instead of him going on further, he had turned and circled back. There was two houses between us and the boss man's, and it appeared that Son was trying to get back to Momma. She was his sister and he was trying to make it to her. So anyhow, the dogs, they caught him. They lynched him on a hill side of the road in Cuthbert. They told us theirselves. They used to ask you what was your last request, and his last request was for them to take his picture and send it to his sister. And they thought that was the greatest thing on earth to do. So they took his picture. A little later on, after we'd heard that he was dead and they'd just wrapped him in a sacking sheet and put him in the dirt, Uncle James went to the law and the law made them dig him up and put him in a box and bury him. They had wanted to kill Uncle James too, but he told them he was going to stay right there and that he guaranteed the ones who had anything to do with Son's lynching wouldn't live twelve months. Those folks dropped out like flies, too. Even the girl who they said Son had flirted at. It must've have been on her mind, because she didn't live long after Uncle James buried Son's body.

And so Uncle James, he left there. After that, Momma got a picture by letter in the mail. I mean, the picture came in the mail and Momma fell. I will never forget that day. Momma was coming home from the white folks' place, where she'd gone to get some meat. She had the meat in her hands, and stopped at the mailbox to get the mail. She looked at it, and saw Son up on that tree. She fainted. Poppa and them had to tote her home. That picture was not shown to Momma any more.

I used to have that picture. And one day while I lived in the Harlem section on St. Simons, a white man came by taking pictures. In those days they would come by and take your picture and carry them off to develop them, put them in a frame, then bring them back. I went and got Son's picture and asked that man to enlarge it for me and he said he would. When he came back, he brought the picture just as he'd carried it away and said he couldn't enlarge that picture. If he did they'd put him in jail, because another man's face was in the photograph too. One day later on, while I was washing and hanging up clothes, a car stopped and two great big rough-looking white men got out. They talked foreign-like and I thought they were fortune tellers or something. Anyway, one of them came up and offered me some money for that picture. I wasn't sure what to do so I told them to wait until they came back another time. Then I told Ms. Perry—the lady I was working for down at Bloody Marsh—and she said to please not give it to them because they were foreigners, and with the war going on that was evidence they might use against the U.S.A. So I didn't give it to them. Some time later I gave the picture to a friend when he said he would enlarge it for me, and I haven't seen it since. I've heard, though, that that picture was shown in Germany! People do take advantage of you—especially when you don't know.

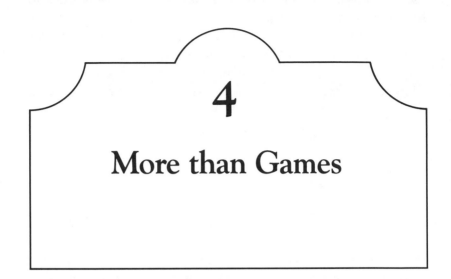

# 4

# More than Games

MY MOTHER'S FATHER was a dark, medium-sized man and wore earrings in his ear. He was brought from Africa for a slave, and was on a plantation in Virginia when freedom came. Many planters then were recommending hands to their friends and asking them to come and get them, and Pa was brought from Virginia to Georgia by a family known as the Dillards. Most of the games I know he taught me. On the plantation in Virginia the slaves used to have many of these games, some of them brought from Africa and others made up right there.

In those days the games were done in different ways on different plantations and each one had its meaning, which most of the slaves knew. But the great mixing up of people after freedom caused a mixup in the games, and changes in the meanings in some ways. Many of the games used to be what you call "talking to the white man in song." Like where my grandfather was in Virginia, they used to have the slaves eat out of a trough on Sundays. They used to have a big thing where they would bring mush from all the houses around and put it in there, then add all the leftovers from through the week, and sometimes fresh roasted rabbit or pig, and gather the slaves around to play games and eat that food. That way they tried to sneak the stuff off them that

44

they brought from Africa. But like the song "Jibber"—people say Juba, but it's really jibber—

> Jibber this, and jibber that
> Jibber kill the alley cat

that's where that song come from. Jibber was the ends of food that they used to have in that trough. They were talking to those folks:

> I sift your meal
> You give me the husk
> Cooked the bread
> You gimme the crust
> I fried the meat
> You gimme the skin
> And that's where Momma's trouble begin. . . .

See, they were talking to them. "And get over double trouble," that was "Someday I'll get to cook my own food." These games were for talking to them white folks direct, because the slaves didn't like the way they were being treated.

Like "Step It Down," that's the title of a song they made up because they had to make bricks in those days. They made bricks with their hands, and it used to be that lots of times people would be working and they'd get too quiet—it's not good to get so quiet when you work. They told us that many times. It makes you worry, then you get to being dissatisfied. Just saying something or doing something helps to make you jolly and get the hardship off of your mind. So they sang songs to get the pressure off their minds. And with "Down in the Brickyard," that's "Step It Down," they were talking to them then. "Someday I hope you remember me; you're not paying me nothing, I'm not getting anything at all, but someday maybe you'll remember me."

If you go to Williamsburg right now you can see those bricks in the street; they were made back then. And anybody with common sense would have known what it meant. They made them bricks, and they'd dance to it to keep the white folks from thinking exactly what they were talking about—

> Way down yonder in the brickyard
> Remember me

> Way down yonder in the brickyard
> Remember me

then they'd dance

> Oh step it, step it, step it down
> Remember me
> Oh step it, step it, step it down
> Remember me
> Now turn your love and swing her around
> Remember me
> Just turn your love and swing her around
> Remember me.

Then they'd clap that and go on to singing it, but they were talking to those white folks: "You've gone on and such, but someday you're gonna remember how you've been treating me." That's while they were using their feet to put the bricks down. So they did all that to get it off their brains, just like eating all the jibber food. When they were talking to them about that, they felt good. Sometimes, Pa said, they'd just laugh at the white folks 'cause they'd tell them, "Do it again. Y'all are so pretty!"

And he said they went to the graveyard many a Sunday to take care of the white folks' children when white folks were being buried. They would see how the white folks were being buried and they would see how they were being buried. So in those days, they had those things they call a "boneyard," where if a cow or a hog or a mule would die, they would carry it down to the edge of the woods and leave it for the buzzards. And Pa and them would watch the buzzards do it, and then they made the buzzard dance, which is called the buzzard lope. They learned that buzzard dance and they could do it pretty! Anyhow, Pa said they'd seen how the white folks were buried and they knew how they were buried, and in their minds they talked it over and thought they might just as well be carried down there and put on the side of the woods so the buzzards could pick the meat off their bones than be buried like they buried them. So this is why they made up the song "Throw me anywhere, Lord." They were talking to the white folks: "You might as well throw me out in that old

46

field, 'cause you ain't doing me right nohow." 'Cause, he said, when white folks buried their dead they had a coffin, a pretty coffin made with style. And when they put the top on it, and entered it down, he said, they'd be acting very nice about it, like they thought something of it. But for us, it was "Here now, take these boards and make him a good box." Yeah, make him a good box. They'd give them a saw and the nails and they had to make it. They'd make that good old rough box and put him in there and that's the way they buried him. He said sometimes the dead would be so full of blood until they couldn't even put on any other clothes: had to wrap them up in sheets in all that blood from they done beat them to death. They beat black men to death in the jailhouse.

Pa's brother tried to burn himself up in one of those jailhouses. That was Uncle Jesse, and they had him buckled to the floor, because he only had one hand. He was a grown man; he didn't want to be treated to all that punishment, you see. So he asked to smoke—he came here smoking from over there—and they gave him his pipe and tobacco and what-have-you. He just had one hand and his feet were buckled but he lit the tobacco, then used the lit tobacco to start a fire in his clothes. He just wanted to burn up, but they smelt the smoke and ran back there. It burned his chest very badly, and he had to stay in the hospital a while.

Now about the clapping: we clap our hands and whether it's in church or anywhere else, they're on time. 'Cause if you clap off-beat it's just—like the Bible say—like taming a salmon. It's no good. You knock others off their beat and singing. So we're like that. Pa and them would clap and get to set-dancing, and they'd do "The Sand," "The Buzzard Lope," and other dances like that, clapping themselves and getting into it. They did the lope dance to keep the people from understanding the buzzard lope song they were singing. But they were talking to them, that's what they were doing. And they made up something that kept old massa and old missus from knowing directly what they were talking about. And it would be funny to them, because the whites would come out there doing that dance, and the tune, trying to see how good they could sing that song. They didn't know what they were talking about. And in doing the dance, doing the buzzard lope, they would spread something out—like an old shirt or a hat—and they had a way of coming down to this thing. The main buzzard, he comes down, looks around, picks around, jumps over it, then he gives out that "Caawww!" and the rest of them come down and they all dance around. Pa and them marked how the buzzards did it and they did it the same way, and it was funny to them to have the white folks doing the dance, because in it folks were telling them

> Throw me anywhere Lord
> In that old field
> Throw me anywhere Lord
> In that old field
> Don't care where you throw me
> In that old field
> Since King Jesus hold me
> In that old field
> Throw me anywhere Lord
> In that old field
> Throw me anywhere Lord
> In that old field
> You may beat and bang me
> In that old field
> Since King Jesus saved me
> In that old field.

Look like people could see it, don't it? But they couldn't see it. And they would dance it. They would dance around the thing and finally they would pick it up. In those days they would pick it up with their mouths, but now you can't get a child to pick it up with his mouth because he'd turn head over heels. They're too weak now. I've tried it and some of those children bucked clean onto the floor, so you got to let them pick it up with their hands—a buzzard ain't got no hands—and then they hold it and act like they're eating it. But that's what the old folks did; they'd pick it up with their mouths and all of them would bring it up and gobble a piece like they were eating.

I know "Little Sally Walker Sitting in a Saucer" about three different ways. Pa used to tell us about Little Sally Walker. There's many times way back, he said, when a white woman—many of them were terrors—saying that "he winked at me" or "he whistled at me" caused many negro boys and men to get killed. And many times they would weep over it, cry over it. That old white woman is Little Sally Walker. And she was crying and weeping over all she had done. You a Negro, you ain't done nothing to cry and weep over. And so Pa said that many a time a white woman would have compassion with the colored people, and wouldn't want the boss man to treat them like that, and would cry. He had seen the white man shove the white woman back and tell her she must have loved that nigger. And she'd be saying, "Don't do them that-a way; don't do them that-a way." And she would cry, weep over it 'cause she didn't like it. Some didn't care, but anyway they done it; they had to weep. So Little Sally Walker is a white woman. Because all the way through, the only slaves there were was a white woman and a negro man. She was a slave and he was a slave. But a white man and a negro woman never been slave. Never have. She could cook and stay there in the house until two o'clock in the morning with those children and he would carry her home. But a negro man couldn't do anything like that with a white woman. That's all there is to it.

And then, right today, in all this good work, all this machinery work and anything that they could keep a Negro out of, then they want that negro man out of it. Course, step by step we're climbing; we're coming on. But we haven't got authority over what we need to have. And Negroes started almost everything you see, from the steam up. Negro man started it; white man took it. Negro boys started the telephone with little tin cans and the white man took it. And instead of pulling him up where he can work, they put him out quick as they see it's something they want. The negro man made the first can-cutter, and all them kinds of things. So with everything the negro man did, if the white man got it he kept it because we have the best. And I'd tell it anywhere anytime just like I'm telling it now, makes me no difference. We're Ethiopians, and Christ is of the Ethiopian tribe.

Mary's daddy was a black man; her mother was a Jew. And so on. But it doesn't really matter 'cause Jesus loves us all. And the song, they made us a different song.

My grandfather used to sing a song about "I'm rolling under, give me the gourd to drink water"—in those days we had to drink water from a gourd. In that song Pa taught us many a day, there's a verse that says

> I've never seen the likes since I've been born
> The bull cow kicking off the milk cow's horn.

They had pastures in those days, and quite naturally we tended the cows out there. And Pa would say, "Chillun, y'all know that bull not gon kick off that milk cow's horns out there in that pasture." Say, "We talking about the white man, see." Then he'd show us how it works. The negro man is the milk cow; the white man is the bull cow. He kept his horns kicked off. He kept him hewed down in every respect. His voice was even kicked off to where he couldn't speak up for himself or nothing. So you see, that's the bull cow. The Negro did all the hard work, all the underground work to start and build a home here. He put all that down, then the white man say, "You get outa the way, nigger; I'm going to decorate it." Then, "I built it," he says. "I built it." And the negro man done did all the hard work, all the underground work, and got the foundation laid down. And they know it. So that's what that song meant. The Lord is so good! I'd say, "Pa, would they know that you were talking about them?" "No," he'd say, "they ain't got sense enough." He said one time, say, "All a white man's brain is up in the top of his head. You see where he gets bald quick? To keep that colored man down he just has to scratch it all out." He'd just have fun saying that. So anyway, all those songs that they made that way, they were very good about them because they were talking directly to them and the white folks didn't know it.

After slavery, my grandfather said, he and the others used to talk to one another about how they should live. How they should do it. They had some hard times, but they'd get together at church or they could talk in their homes together. They'd have a

50

council on Sundays—it had to be on Sundays because they had to work hard right on the rest of the week—and they'd sit down and talk things over. But, Pa said, there were some of them right then you couldn't talk to. You talk to them here and the next thing you know they done told out yonder. Done told ol' massa. Course there wasn't any more massa, but slavery went along a good while after they called freedom, and it's still going on yet. Because we are yet under them white folks' name. We got a slave name. And they know our name. They got a background and they know it's up there.

Once when we were at Williamsburg, Virginia, making a movie, I told them there about Uncle Jesse trying to burn himself up in the jail, and they let me see the jail. I was glad to be there because this is where my grandfather came from to Georgia. That night they asked me to sing a song for babies—a lullaby. It was at a birthday party and we had to dress up in their costumes. I had on a dress look like my grandmother used to wear—with those long wide shirts and whole lot of underskirts—and I was delighted to put it on. We went there to sing together, but God works in mysterious ways. Before we started they asked me to sing this lullaby for the baby's birthday; I think Lomax had told them how much I like children, I don't know. But when I got up, I said I was glad to do it because this is where my grandfather was brought up at, and that gave me a head to speak right there. When I said that, they stopped the beer right there, and everything, and I was getting ready to sing to the child, but wasn't nobody saying nothing. Then something told me, "You got to tell them everything in your mind." It was at the Queen's house. The waitress and manager just stood there 'cause nobody wasn't taking anything. They were looking straight at me.

So then I told them, "When I see that trough out there," I told them, "I think about what my grandfather said. He said that if I ever came here I would see the trough that he used to eat out of." I just poured it like it was ice out of a can but I had to tell them that. I said, "And my grandfather said that they had to eat from that trough on a Sunday and they be playing games that they had learned in Africa. When I see that straw—the broom straw—I

51

recall my grandfather had to jump over the broom to marry my grandmother right here during slavery times. And that long iron with pigs and things roasting on it, that's how they fixed the food for the wedding dinners and things right here. I see them gourds hanging up all out there and it makes me think about how he said they had to drink water from a gourd; he had us drinking also from a gourd when we were coming up. And he told me if I ever come here to ask the people to show me the jailhouse my granduncle tried to burn himself up in." Wasn't a soul saying a word but me, and I just told them like it was. There was a big old white man there, and he asked me, say, "What was your grandmother's name before she married?" I said, "I don't know." I didn't know, but that was the only question they asked me. So we went on and carried the program out that night.

The next day, around one o'clock, they called down to the hotel where we were staying and told me to come up there. And so I went up there to see what they wanted. When I got there, the man escorted me through, said, "I want to show you something." There are big books in there that done got brown-looking. And he turned the leaves and he showed me the history of the whole crew from the time they came over here. And that was great to me. Then he took me to the jailhouse and showed me that they had the same slant table there that Pa and them used to talk about, where they used to buckle you down by your hands and feet and beat you. And in that book they had the history of many of our grandfathers and great-grandfathers, if only we knew which one to ask for.

I went not too long ago on tour to a place called Dillard, Georgia, and I was surprised! That name rung a bell with me deeply because I was brought up on a plantation called Dillard's Place. But the Dillards I knew came from north Georgia. There was one man there at the program old enough to know Miss Susan Dillard, and he said, "Nothing around here much but Dillards." He said they were from Dawson. Next day after the program a white man came up and told me, say, "I work for Miss Edith and I'm looking for the singer." So Guy Carawan—I was touring with him—got up and asked, "What's happened?" He said, "We were talking last night after the program and I want to see the lady that was brought up at Dillard's Place." He said, "I want to show you something." And so, I went up to the house with him, and Guy went with me. They had a long, wide book there from their great-grandfather's plantations up around Dawson and other places in there. And in there were all the grandfathers and great-grandfathers from slavery. Mr. Thomas, Mr. Carter, Mr. Shaw, and my grandfather: they were all in that book. I'm telling you, that was something! Those people were moved by our program and they sat up there and said they were going to make a monument for me. That's funny. But I thank God for it. I ain't got nowhere to run 'cause everything out there, I came up with it. And the Lord blessed me not to forget these things and keep them up among people who weren't studying it. White people know our background, but they're going to try to hold it back and keep us back as long as they possibly can.

When Pa and them sang about the rolling under and the drinking water from a gourd, he said that they wanted them to know, if they could see it, that they got them rolling under at all times and in everything. They had to wait until the white folks bought a bolt of cloth and made it up. Made shirts, dresses, and little children's clothing: everything with that one piece of cloth. And white folks thinking that they were so good to them, treating them good. But they were rolling under sure as they had been born, because they couldn't get things the way they wanted them. Couldn't do it like they wanted, because after slavery they were working out for wages so they could buy little things. So Pa said that they would get together and they would talk, "Now let's try to climb. Let's try to do better." The way to do better was to treat one another better: love one another. But some of them had that slave mentality deep in them. They beat their children just like ol' massa used to beat them. And that made the children run away from home.

See, a boy wasn't grown in those days until he reached twenty-one, and a girl at twenty or twenty-two. When a boy turned twenty-one, then he could wear long pants. Before that he wore knee pants. The first long pants my Uncle Bill put on, he left that same day and ran off with a show. He was a great buck dancer and a big show was there. He joined that show the same day. But Pa followed that show down—he had intentions of following it as long as he had to—for two days from Dawson to Fort Gaines, and when he caught up with it, he didn't even know Uncle Bill. They had Bill disguised in the show. But Bill saw Pa, and said he didn't want Pa to go back without him, because he knew that Pa was looking for him. So he came out and he took Pa's hand, and came back home. But they just weren't grown until twenty-one, see. So Pa said they made a game—and I played it sometimes—called "Down in the Valley." And they'd show us how to get down on our knees together, or else squat down, and we're down in the valley two by two. Sometimes the whole ring would get down in the valley. But it showed that if you're down now, you know you're down, rise! And after you rise don't stand there: some folks, you would help them up and they ain't moving; you have to go there and move them. They're just there. Next time you see them they done flopped down again, 'cause they ain't moving and they ain't trying to get nowhere. And so that's what he was showing you. If you get up, then try to do something. And when you do something, do something else. And when you're doing something and begin to accumulate a little something, help somebody else. So that's where they get their partners from: down in the valley two by two. And another song says, "Rise, Sally, rise," it says, "let me see you make a motion." You got to do something, and when you do that it says, "Let me see you make another one." And now you choose somebody to help you do it. So that way, the game is teaching you to do right and to help someone, but if you don't do no good, don't do any harm. And that's where "Na Na" come in: "Na Na Thread Needle." He taught us that game in many a day. Say, that's a direct thing as they come out from under slavery and they played these games to show us that it doesn't matter what you do, some people are not going to do right. Pa said, you can give them cake and chicken every day, and hand pie crust to them; they ain't going to do right. It's got to be in your heart, he said many times; it's got to be in there before it could come out. And so he taught us the game "Na Na Thread Needle."

In this game the teaching is, when people borrow and don't pay back, don't get angry. Wind it up with love. We line everybody up side by side from the tallest to the smallest, and holding hands in upright position like windows. The tallest hollers down to the smallest:

>Neighbor loan me your hatchet

and the reply:

>Neighbor, neighbor, step and fetch it.

The caller says:

>Na Na

and everybody answer:

>Thread needle.

Then the tallest turns and goes under his left arm and everybody follows until the last person turns. Then they stretch out again, and the smallest hollers,

>Neighbor, neighbor, send me my hatchet.

Naturally, that leads to argument. Until the small one says:

>Well I'm getting tired of this
>I'm gonna wind up this borrowing.

Tallest one says

>Go ahead, wind it up. I don't care.

And everybody sings:

>I'm gonna wind up this borrowing
>I'm gonna wind up this borrowing

turning and winding up around the tallest. Then you jump softly and sing:

>Shake down this borrowing
>Unwind this borrowing

as you unwind.

Most of what I know come from my ancestors. Good Christian people, most of them were. For instance, Pa taught us many things that were right from the teachings of Jesus. Like about borrowing and lending. Pa used to say that rather than to fall out with a person about borrowing and lending, you should wind it up with love, and separate with love. Patch it up. Because, he told us, and I know that this is the truth, if you fall out with people about owing you and not paying you, as long as you live you'll be falling out with people, 'cause you're always going to find somebody that's not going to do right. If you work for them, sometimes, then they won't pay you. Then sometimes they borrow your stuff and get mad at you and tell folks they never borrowed nothing from you, and all that kind of thing. But when you know you've done right, you know you done the best you could for them, just don't go fighting them 'cause then you'd be just as bad as them or worse. Some folks say, "You gonna give me my so-and-so; you gonna give me my thing back!" and all that kind of mess. I just let it alone: but you don't get no more. See, that's the end of it.

My grandfather used to show us how to do by telling stories: like the story about something happened back then in slavery time. There was a white man, he acted like a Christian man in a way, and didn't like to beat his slaves if they got sick. Instead, he was very kind to them. When one man found out this owner wasn't going to work him sick and wasn't going to beat him, he stayed sick. Pa say his name was Medium. His wife was named Mary. So Medium stayed sick, and stayed sick. He stayed at home while Mary was out working. And sometimes when she came home, all the peas and things she'd left warming in the pot on the fireplace, Medium had already eaten the whole pot and everything. He's at home.

The man who owned the place was so nice: he'd tell the other hands to go and see Medium before they got off for the night, and those people would come to Medium's house to sing and pray with him, but Medium always had the same song—"I'm so sick, I'm so-ooo sick, just waiting til the Lord come and get me, ooh children, I'm sooo sick, just waiting on the Lord, child."

The owner even had a doctor to visit Medium, and when the doctor came he'd go along and give Medium a little something, because in those days doctors didn't know what they know now.

Medium stayed sick like that near about two years, until one old white man from another plantation told the owner of the place, say, "You think that nigger is sick?" "Yes, he's sick." "You ought to shake him up." "No, no," the owner got kind of provoked. "I wouldn't hit him. I don't do that." "I didn't mean hit him, I mean shake him up: scare him. And you'll find out whether he's sick or not." "You mean not hurt him or anything like that?" "No. We can fix a way to scare him and see if he really is sick or not."

On that plantation there was no white horse, or mule, or anything like that. So they went and borrowed a white horse from another plantation. Mary and Medium's house sat right side of the road near a white sand bed and a white sycamore tree. They waited for a night of full moon, when the moon shines all night real bright, and they got a young white boy about nineteen, Pa said, and put him on this white horse. The boy came in a white suit, white shoes, and a white flour sack starched stiff setting up on his head like a crown. They told that boy what to do.

That night the people came to see Medium as usual, and in his bed Medium say, "Ooh, I'm so sick, children; I'm so sick; I don't see how I'm going to stand it. I can't stand it. I'm just waiting on the Lord, I'm just waiting here oh Lord, come get me." So after everybody done prayed and left, Mary's sitting by the fireplace, and Medium is back there laying on the bed, done eat and everything, his belly full, they heard somebody out in the yard. The voice said, "Woah."

Mary sat up because she knew that nobody came around their house at that hour of the night. The voice said, "Hello!" She heard it again, "Hello!" So Mary said, "Who's there?" The voice said, "It's me Mary, the Lord. I've come for Medium." When Medium heard that he said, "Mary, what did it say?" She said, "It's a ghost. A ghost must have come for you."

"Medium!" the voice said. "Medium, you better come out

here." Mary was scared, and Medium was scared. The voice said again, "Medium!" Medium said, "Mary, you go." The voice said, "I want you, Medium."

Medium said he ain't going. Then the voice said, "Well Mary, I can't go alone so I guess I'll have to carry you."

"No, ghost!" she said. "I ain't waiting on you, Medium is. I ain't holding you, ghost." And she called, "Medium!" By that time, Medium was up under the bed. "Medium, come from underneath that bed," she said. "You come from under that bed. I ain't waiting on no ghost, it come for you."

"Medium, I can't wait any longer," the voice said. "If you don't come out, I'm coming in."

Mary opened the door and shouted, "Here he is!"

And Medium, "Get back, Mary! Get back out of the door! The Lord got to catch me tonight!" And with that Medium bolted out that door.

The moon was shining bright, there wasn't a house or nothing nearby, and the boy waited until Medium got a good ways up the road, then turned the horse around and came riding after him, and that man was gone! He ran clear out of sight; it took two days to catch up with Medium. They found out whether he was sick or not.

Pa used to tell us that story to let us know we shouldn't play sick.

And he used to tell us about another character—his name was John. There are a lot of stories about John, but this one was pointed to be true. John was this man who worked about the master's house all the time, and a lot of colored people who worked in the fields didn't like John having it easy around the house all the time so they would pimp on John. They would lie on him. And that caused old massa to beat John and treat him bad. They would steal things, and say John moved it. They made it hard on John and he finally got tired of it.

He used to get around with the master when they went to church, so he heard about God and hell, and being as the master treated him so bad he didn't want God to do anything for the master or his family. So the best thing he thought to do was pray for the devil to come and get them.

John had to get up early every morning and feed the mules before breakfast, and one morning the master wanted him to give the mules extra feed because he wanted some hard work out of them that day, so he went out there to tell John and John wasn't there. He pulled the window open on John's little room and John wasn't there. He went back to the kitchen where his wife was cooking breakfast and told her. He asked her what she thought he should do. He said, "I called and called, I whistled, and still don't know where he's at. I guess I'll whip him." His wife said, "Don't beat him; just watch and see where he is." They thought John was stealing somewhere.

So the next morning the master went to the lot soon before John, hoping he was gonna catch him stealing. John came down there, whistling like he always did, and when he got through feeding the mules he looked towards the house, didn't see ol' massa or nobody, and then he made a bee-line down to the woods behind the garden. The master followed. When the master got there, John was in the graveyard bowed down praying—"Oh Debbie"—he called the devil Debbie—"Oh Debbie, I want you to come and git ol' massa; git ol' massa and massa's wife, the overseer, and the overseer's wife. Debbie, ol' massa treat me so bad, come git ol' massa, Debbie."

When the master heard, he went back to his wife and said, "Old John is down in the graveyard praying for the devil to come and get us. I'm gonna kill him. I'm gonna beat him till his guts fall out." She said, "Uh, uh! Don't kill him. He don't know no better; don't beat him. The thing you do is you go out to the barn with him every morning and stay out there with him until he gets through feeding up and then he can't do that." She had a good heart. So the master thought he would do that.

But later that day, he told some more people about old John praying for the devil to come and get them, and one old white man said, "Listen, you better do something to stop that nigger 'cause he means it. And if the devil don't hear him, God will."

At that, they began to get scared, and put their heads together to find out what to do. The old white man said, "Now if you go out to that lot like you plan to that ain't gonna stop him from praying. He's gonna pray right on." So they made them a plan to make John think the devil came as he asked for. They got a big sheet and dyed it black, then they cut holes in it for the eyes and nose, then they made a crown with some long red horns. Massa was a tall man, and with the crown on he looked even taller. Then they made a triangle with the corner behind and at each side, and put a stake up in each corner on the sides to make it look like wings. So this was a big black thing with the holes in it, and this red crown with long red horns, it was a dangerous-looking thing. So massa's the devil.

The next morning before day, ol' massa went down to the graveyard and hid behind some bushes from where he could see John come in, and where John was going to go. John came down. He didn't know massa was there and done seen him. So he went down to the grave and pulled off his cap, he got down and went to praying—"Oh Debbie, please Debbie, I want you to come git ol' massa, ol' massa's wife, overseer, and overseer's wife. Debbie, ol' massa don't believe nothing I say. Oh Debbie, come git ol' massa; Debbie, please come git ol' massa, Debbie."

And a voice said, "Ummmm."

John stopped—"Debbie?"

"Ummmmm."

That time John looked up and just then massa eased out of the bushes with his wings flapping just a little bit. "Debbie, that you Debbie?" John said.

Massa say, "Uh huh," and came a little closer.

"Debbie, you coming at ol' massa?"

"Nooooo."

John backed off, "You coming at ol' massa's wife?"

"Nooo," and he came a little closer.

"Debbie, you coming at the overseer?"

"Uh, uh." He was close enough then for John to see everything. He said, "Debbie, you come at me?"

"Uh huh." John dropped his cap and took off and he was in

Baltimore when they found him again. The master didn't mean to get rid of him and somebody finally turned him over, but John never prayed to the devil no more.

Pa used to tell us that story, and when he did I could just see the devil. It was sad for John. But those folks back then were in bad shape with all that hardship they had to go through. They didn't know which way to go. What could they do? They had an old-time song they used to moan.

> I done done all I could do
> What more could I do, Lord
> Lord I done done all I could do
> And I can't hold out.

That is real, and something to think about. They mean't that; they didn't know what to do. Looked like they did everything to get along, and nothing they did done any good. So those folks were going through some hardships, and all those good songs, and the meanings of those songs, the Lord gave it to them. It was handed down to them without any schooling. And that's why I have been so delighted to keep it going the old way—the way they had it.

Pa taught me a lot of riddles and a lot of stories about what happened in slavery to different ones, and some of it was fun and some of it was sad. I still tell them. Of course there were some that they tried to keep from us, but my cousin and me, when we were supposed to be asleep in the other room, we would listen to them and eavesdrop while they would say things that they wouldn't tell before us, and so we learnt it. And me, myself, being like I was, with a little help I'd just remember it and we'd go out and do it again.

Huckleberry doesn't have any other name, but the gooseberry, some folks call them blueberries. But we call them gooseberries. Now the huckleberry is smaller and black but they're round and sweet, and look like a sugar berry. The sugar-berry tree grows to be real big, though, and the story is told about the elephant and the sugar-berry tree.

A long time ago when this world began—we don't know a

thing about it, and the first one to tell this story got it from a book—but anyway, they say that man was down here and they planted nice gardens and everything and the rabbit and other animals used to go back and forth on a chariot. So the rabbit told the Lord one day, say, "You know what?" he was sharp. Always been sharp. "I want to be your door-minder."

The Lord said, "You do?"

"Yeah; I want to mind the door for you. I'll mind it."

The Lord said, "Alright. I'll tell you what you do; I'm going to give you three tests, and if you pass the three tests then I'll let you be a door-minder."

"Alright, alright," the rabbit said. He was pleased, because as door-minder he would get to know who came in and who went out.

The Lord said, "Now, I'm going to let you down on earth and I want you to bring me back a crockersack full of rattlesnakes."

"Sure, sure. Alright."

So He let rabbit down, where the rattlesnakes were just crawling around on one another. A pool of them. Rabbit looked at those ugly things and he was scared of them. But he went up there, and since back then every animal could understand one another he said, "Hey! Hey!" to the rattlesnakes. "You know what? Everybody's talking about y'all."

"What?" the rattlesnakes were surprised.

"Everybody's talking about y'all; say you ain't got no sense."

"No sense?"

"You ain't got a bit of sense—ain't got enough sense to crawl in this sack."

"Yes we do," and they crawled in there. Rabbit twisted the mouth of that sack around and signaled he was ready to come up.

When he got up there the Lord said, "You did get them, I see."

"Yeah. I got them."

"Alright. Now you go back, and bring me a sack full of blackbirds." And he let rabbit down where there were plenty of blackbirds.

Rabbit told the blackbirds the same story:: "You ain't got no sense. You can't even fly in this sack. I'm going to open it and I bet you can't, 'cause everybody says you're crazy." So the blackbirds flew in and filled up the sack. Rabbit took them on back up there.

He said, "Here they are."

The Lord said, "Alright. You got one more test. I want you to go back down and bring me a cup of elephant milk."

Rabbit had never seen an elephant before, and when he did it frightened him. He looked at it; he danced. He looked at it, and thought how was he going to get that milk? And then he saw a little bird up in a sugar-berry tree. This was a huge tree with lots of sugar berries, but they weren't ripe. They don't fall when they're not ripe. So rabbit got to studying and finally he said, "Hey, bird! You see that big old rough-looking thing over there?"

"The elephant?"

"Yeah, the elephant."

"Yeah."

"Let's have some fun with it."

"How?"

"I'll tell you what to do," rabbit said. "I'm going to run against the tree and butt it. When I bump the tree, you pick the berries and just let them fall. I'm going to tell that elephant that big as he is, I'm stronger. Now when he runs and butts against the tree, don't let any berries fall. But when I butt against it, let them come down. We'll have fun." The bird didn't know that for fun but he got with rabbit anyway.

Rabbit walked up to the elephant. "Hey, Mr. Elephant, how you do?"

"Alright."

"I tell you one thing though, big lady, you're big but you ain't stronger than me."

"I bet I am," the elephant said.

"I bet you one thing. See that tree yonder? I bet you I can shake berries out of that tree and you can't."

The elephant just laughed and said, "Little as you are? Let me see you shake those berries down."

Rabbit went way back and run up to the tree, and bumped the tree, boom! Berries came falling down. That tickled the elephant. She went back and came up to the tree, boom! No berries.

"Get on out of the way," rabbit said, "I told you I was stronger." He backed off and bumped the tree again and berries came shooting down. That made the elephant mad. So she went back, way back. She got him a hard gallop and she hit that tree. When she hit the tree her head went in there, and while she was trying to get her head out, rabbit ran up and milked her. Alright. Time to go up. God called him up. He put the milk down.

The Lord said, "Alright. You know what you did? You went down there and you lied all the way through. You lied to the rattlesnakes, you lied to the birds, and you tricked the elephant."

That made rabbit mad, because he didn't know that God knew what he had done. So he sucked his teeth at God. He turned his back and sucked his teeth at God and God chunked the milk at him and that made his tail white. That's why rabbit got a white tail today. And there's enough in real life to show how this works, too.

A man told me one time up in North Carolina, he said, a lady from Georgia—one of them that hustles money out of men—she went around with him. He said he messed around there, and before he knew anything he had spent about three hundred dollars on that woman. Alright. He spent it. Just about that time she got to acting up, went bucking out with somebody else, saying, "He's my sucker," and he heard it. A lot of men would have cut her throat and left her body lying one way and her head another, but he didn't. He looked into it. He thought, now she thinks she's got me going but I'm going to let her go right now. That good thing didn't go any further. He dropped her right then. When he did, all the money she had was soon gone and somebody had already stolen part of the nice clothes she had bought. And what now? He tipped his hat to her whenever he saw her. He told us about it privately, because he didn't want everybody around there to know that he had been a big sucker. But he said, "Now she thinks she's done something but she's going to need more." Then she went to falling from door to door, see, 'cause that other man she had didn't have that kind of money to give her. This guy had big things. He had fourteen milk cows, and put his milk out there to the road every day; eggs going to town all the time; potatoes, tomatoes, all that good stuff. He was a negro man, had hands in the field working for him all the time. She hadn't touched his pocket, that's what tickled him so bad. He said, "If I'da kept on with her, I would've messed up," because he'd had it in his mind to buy her a little corner lot to build her a house on. And there she was, getting off on that three hundred dollars. She ain't got nowhere.

So Pa said, it shows you that some people ain't going to do right. He told us that many times; some folks think you're a sucker because you treat them right and they pop around and do you wrong. When you find them out, tell them "No more."

I had reason to recall what Pa taught me about folks thinking you're a sucker because you treat them right. I was treated like that once in Miami and it was a while before I found out. I left Georgia and went down to Miami in 1926, and met some people there from Georgia, and that done me good to meet folks from home, and some direct from places I had been. I thought that was just alright. And I became friends, because I was taught that way. Never take a buddy woman, but have a woman friend. You need a woman to do things that a man can't sometimes, but your main secrets, if you got any, don't put them out there. Not to a woman. If you're going to have anybody, have a buddy man. I learnt that to be successful. But anyhow, when this girl and I wanted to go places, I would be delighted. She had a boyfriend with a nice car and we would ride. I didn't want them to be riding me, and since we were friends together and that was her boyfriend, not her husband—she didn't have a husband and I didn't then either—I'd buy the gas all the time whenever we went, and pay for the set-ups. I wasn't much on dancing but I used to play cards for fun—not gambling—or for the get-up, as we called it. We'd play two best out of three, and whoever lost had to get up. Well one day a lady told me about it, that this child was saying that I was a big sucker. Said any time they wanted to go somewhere, I paid the gas and I bought the drinks.

I was their sucker. I got so mad, I told her, say, "Don't you ever come around me no more. If I'm your sucker then you go find you another one but don't you never come around me no more." When I told her, she cried. She didn't know they were going to tell it but it was true; she said it.

Another while I was working as a maid for some white folks but I kept me a separate room. I ain't never wanted to stay in no white folks' house with all my stuff there, because if we should fall out, then I knew I got some place to go. So I paid my rent and kept my little room. I had an upstairs room but I used to cook downstairs in the kitchen. So anyway, every morning, time for breakfast, here came two of them that I had been friends with. And we sat and we ate and then I got dressed to go to work. I was working for a white lady who was on a diet and I didn't have to cook breakfast for her. The kids would be going to school by the time I got there, so I could eat my home breakfast, then go on and do my work all day until the kids came in. About two or three months went by; then Percy, a Nassau man who ran the house where I was renting, said, "I want to tell you something. Them gals ain't doing a thing but riding you, you know." I didn't know how to take it. I said, "What d'you mean?" He said, "They come right in here and they eat breakfast with you every morning, then they go around at somebody else and eat in the afternoon." Said, "They're jumping one and hopping two. They're just living off of you, that's all."

I had trouble seeing into that, because I wasn't used to such junk. But it worked on my mind while I was on the job and I thought he might be telling the truth. So the next morning they came again. When they came in, it bumped me sure enough what he had said, but I didn't say anything. I just let them talk right on, but decided to try something and see if he was telling the truth. So that same day I went out and bought me a coal bucket. I got some coal in it, and Percy's wife told me how to start the fire, then set the coal bucket in the window until the gas ran off, then set it in the house. I had one of those big dressers. I put my pots and pans in it, my plates and things, my food—the whole dresser was just like a grocery box you might say. That next morning I cooked in my room. I fried my sausages and got my grits while those two were sitting down in the kitchen and I didn't even know they were there. So I had eaten and everything, and was standing to the glass fixing my little hair up, when they came easing up the stairway. They smelled the sausages and the other food when they got up there, but what made me hot was the door was kind of open and they could look in and see me standing at the mirror. They seen the coal bucket and one said, "Ummm! Sharp, ain't it. I see, sharp there." I felt like putting them down that stair with my fist. I looked at the girl and I had to take it easy 'cause I didn't want them to know that I knew anything. "It's sharp, ain't it! Even upstairs sharp, ain't it." They seen that coal bucket with the things in it. "You fixing to go to work?" And I said, "Yes, I'm going to work," and went on. Next morning I wasn't there. I wasn't there at all the next morning, and Percy said they came but he told them, said, "Yeah, you don't run no more. You go on upstairs if you like but I ain't gonna let her give you nothing to eat."

But that's one that got away from me because I wasn't used to such a trick as that. Not at all. But you got to learn: live and learn. I mean, they weren't working anywhere; I'm working: I'm rushing. I like to draw my own money; I don't care what anybody else might be doing. Let me have my own cash. I was in company with a man. He had a nice store and three woodyards. I didn't have to work, but baby, I like my little donation. And my little house. You get in there; you go out. Don't say you're gonna stay there. I am that way, I imagine, because I didn't have a brother and my father never whipped on me. I never had anything like that, and I don't want to be dogged on. I figure you ought to treat me right. If I treat you right you ought to treat me right. But that doesn't go all the time.

So my grandfather taught me all of that coming up. Everybody ain't gonna treat you right, and it takes love and it takes good patience to get along with some people. It's times when you can game them, and times when you can't. Pa said there's no way in this world to sweeten quinine, except with honey. Sugar won't sweeten it; syrup won't sweeten it; but honey will. That's the only thing that will do it.

I never did march at anybody during the days of Martin Luther King, because I didn't believe in marching the streets for things, so I didn't march. But there were nine of us from this section, and we had a prayer band and would go from place to place and pray. Sometimes three or four of us would go, sometimes all of us would go. So we were at a place called Beulah, Mississippi, and Martin and all of them were there, and we read that in the Bible about shaking it off. We thought, there must be some way that we could sing this and make people understand. We wouldn't get anywhere by just putting it into song, because people would say we were singing the blues. So we put that teaching into a ring game there in Mississippi and just let the children shake it off. They just shaked their little hips and things, and the men too, and it was good to let them know what we were talking about. Say,

> Alabama, Mississippi
> Alabama, New Orleans
> Alabama, number one
> You gotta shake, shake, shake, shake it baby
> Shake, shake, shake, shake it baby
> Shake it back to New Orleans.

Then after number one steps back you go to number two, then number three, and on down until you come to everybody. It's really pretty. But the most important thing is that they know what I mean. I tell them before we start. Not the body, 'cause you're gonna shake that anyhow, but your brain, your mind, your understanding, the life you have to live these days. Shake it off.

Then we would do the game "Momma momma kuma momma," and every person has to come out and do a different dance. But some of them come out there and they ain't doing a thing. They get ashamed. Especially the young ones. And I have to explain to them that movements of the body—the hips—is not the whole thing. Your brains, thoughts, and understanding are at play too. And before we get to playing the game I try to explain that when

we way "Shake, shake" that means you got to shake off meanness, dirtiness, madness, hatred, and things like that. Setting
people afire, killing people for nothing, or thinking you're better
than somebody else or somebody else's better than you. You want
to get rid of all that kind of stuff—hating to see somebody wear
something, or eat good. Some folks really hate and have envy.
They don't want to see another get nowhere, and that goes from
the churches on down to the jukes. That goes for all kinds of
people. But in that song, that game, you're supposed to shake it
off. The Bible makes a special announcement about that, and
says before the end of time you got to shake it off. Before the end
of time the Ethiopians—that's us, the black folks—got to shake
off doubt and failure. We doubt because we've been defeated for
so long but we've got to shake that off, and don't study being
mean and dirty 'cause you've got to love people. And if you're
gonna love, you don't need doubt.

Sometimes it happens in a ring the children don't want to clap
one another's hands, and if one goes ahead and catches the other's
hand anyway you see them wiping it off. Black ones don't want
to hold the white ones' hands; white don't want to hold the black
hands; girls don't want to touch boys, acting scornful and all like
that. So I told them one day, say, "You know what's really dirty
and nasty and shouldn't be touched unless you have your hands
cleaned or hold it with a piece of paper?" They said, "What?"
"The doorknob. Your own doorknob. That's the nastiest thing
in the house." I said, "You try it." They looked at one another.
"You try it. You walk in that bathroom and you ain't guaranteed
that the person before you washed. Especially a man. He walks
up there and the first thing he grabs is that doorknob when he's
coming out. You just don't know. You hold that doorknob coming in and out of your house and you don't know what the hand
that held it before you was doing. So if you want to shun anything, you shun that doorknob. You'll find more germs there
than you would in the whole house or on any body." The children
looked at me so funny. But you got to teach them when they're
scorning one another in the wrong way and get them together.

When I was a child living with Grandpa and them we used to

have guineas: speckled chickens with a crown on their heads. We called him a king bird and he mostly is king, too. He's a spiritual bird. He hollers for death and he hollers for somebody around the house, too. Just like a dog may do. They liked to roost in trees and they would leave home too, almost like bees. You get too many wandering around and some will leave to go off and start them a different nest. We had a whole lot of chickens, too, and turkeys. Sometimes the turkeys would go astray and lay their eggs in the woods and people seeing the nests would get the eggs. But sure as you put your hands on a turkey's nest, he ain't going there no more. He wouldn't continue to live there. You're always supposed to go to a turkey's nest with a long spoon and dip the eggs up. When you put your hands in their nests they will find another place, and go way off where you won't be sticking your hands in their nests. Now if you have them in a pen or a coop, then that's different. They can't go out. But if they're loose, they'll show you something. And when the turkeys were off nesting in the woods, we'd have to round them up to get them back and that's where that "Shoo Turkey" game came from. When going to hunt a turkey you gotta walk easy and get around them. Don't race at them. If you do, you ain't gonna outrun them because those scoundrels can run. But you walk easy and come up on them, then shoo them in. Sometimes it would be a whole gang going to round up turkeys, because they'd run off from different people and meet up in the woods and live together. We wouldn't always know which was whose but we'd round them up together, and that would be a part of a game.

Everybody got into a marching line one behind the other and the caller would sing: "Little girls, little boys. . . ."

> Answer:
> Yes ma'am
> Did you go to the barn?
> Yes ma'am
> Did you feed my turkeys?
> Yes ma'am
> Did you get any eggs?
> Yes ma'am

> Did you bring them home?
> Yes ma'am
> Did you give them to your momma?
> Yes ma'am
> Did she put it in the bread?
> Yes ma'am
> Did she give you some?
> Yes ma'am
> Did you save me mine?
> Yes ma'am
> Now is the turkeys gone?
> Yes ma'am
> Which way did they go?
> So, so (pointing fingers)
> Will you help me to find them?
> Yes ma'am
> Get ready, let's go.

And everyone would squat around in a circle fanning the turkeys and singing "Shoo turkey, shoo shoo . . . ." It's a joy to see, especially when the children are small. It's real cute.

It's welcome to sing and it's welcome to say "thank God." It's welcome to sing hallelujah, and amen. I've been knowing hallelujah songs for many years. We had them for when somebody was dead and gone: "You done killed my ma, you done killed my pa, my momma done worked to death and dead now." That's what they would sing about:

> Hallelu, hallelu-hallelu
> Hallelu, hallelu my Lord
> I'm going to see my friends again
> Hallelu.

And there was another way they sang the same song:

> Death come to my house
> It didn't stay long
> I looked on the bed
> My mother was gone
> And I'm going to see my friends again
> Hallelu

and they would walk from one to the other shaking hands:

71

Hallelu, hallelu-hallelu
Hallelu, hallelu my Lord
I'm going to see my friends again
Hallelu.

Now see, they meant that. They meant they wanted to see them again and they had a lot of verses to the song.

Where I grew up we lived close with the spirits those days, and that come from way back. There're all kinds of spirits, some for good and some for bad, but a person should know how to protect theirself. Not everybody who do bad set out meaning to do it. Pa used to tell us that some of our people when they got over here got treated so bad, they didn't know anything about how they would stop the world or how they come into it. A lot of them didn't want to work for the white people for nothing like they were doing, and they wanted something to command the money from the people or make the people help them, you know, something like that, or get over some way, somehow. No education and no understanding and nothing like that, I guess they just wanted to do some underground work, that's all. And so, that's why a lot of them went into witches, see, and they turned theirself into the wrong thing which it would cause them to do something they didn't want to do. But after they do it, Pa say, after you git into that thing, then you got to do it. You can't back off, and then it's just that. And so whatsoever you connected with, then that's what you gonna be. But the best thing to do is just go on and deal with what's facing you. Then you know what you is. In the morning you know where you at, in the evening you know what you're doing and then you know what the devil is saying. You can free it out of you, that's true. You can pray out of a condition. But when you turn witch you can't, 'cause you done sold out.

My Aunt Margaret, who was staying just above us when we were in Fitzgerald, she was a witch. See, a witch rides at night, and Pa said they got to ride something, that's why they get to people's horses and mules and things. I don't know what they call that and I just don't never want to know that stuff. But somehow Aunt Margaret didn't want Momma giving Annie anything. So anyway, Momma had a friend who I think was connected with Momma some way, some kind of kin on the side of her people up there in Smithville, and she had us to call him Uncle Jesse. At one time he'd been real sick, very low. The doctor was looking for him to die, but Momma and them treated him with tea and medicines and things and he got where he could set up and walk around. So one night he sent to see a lady. I think it was a white woman not far across the road where we stayed. Her name was Laura, and they stayed on a plantation too. Anyhow, he'd been over there to see this lady and was on his way coming back home early in the morning when he seen a woman coming ahead of him. This woman had on a long dress, a bouncing long dress, and he looked where that woman was coming and he got up there and met her and he seen it was Aunt Margaret.

He asked her, "Where're you going this time of the morning?" She say, "It's necessary. And don't you tell nobody you seen me." And she say, "Don't you go to the house waking up everybody either, 'cause they ain't gonna wake up until I git back there." And that's when he knew right then that she was something. She say, "Now don't go and try waking up Jim and Abby and them but I be back after a while. And don't tell nobody you seen me." Now that's when they begin to find out really that she was a witch, although Poppa say he had already felt it. He noticed that every time Momma be rid he had a certain feeling about Aunt Margaret, but she used to say it was somebody else around there riding Momma. And so when Uncle Jesse told Momma about it, he way, "You watch her now, 'cause you'll sure see her." Alright.

So one day Lula told me, she say, "Grandma got something in her trunk." Say, "I'm going to show it to you, but Grandma lay everything like she want it and I got to take the thing out myself." They had one of them flat-top trunks, you know, and so Lula taken the thing out and showed me: a little old thing, a little old bone, a fine little bone in there. And so she wouldn't touch it with her hands, she just showed it to me. And she say, "This is what Grandma takes out sometimes, and when she take it out I watch her. And then she go." Now what she do with it, I don't know. I know it was a funny-looking bone. I seen it with my own eyes.

And anyway, after that Poppa and them used to get a sifter—you know, that thing would have to count all them holes—and Pa put it down at the foot of the bed. That thing stayed away for a while but then it had to come. One night it come and he heard it. He say it come near the foot of the bed, then turned right around, then come back up. Momma was sitting on the back of the bed, and in the dark that thing come around right on her side. And so Poppa hauled off and hit at the thing, and he must've hit it, see. It went right on back, and through a hole near the door. So Poppa stopped up that hole. Next day Poppa was going to work—I'll never forget that day as long as I live—and Margaret was standing up in her doorway taking snuff. She was standing there, and Poppa say, "We got a big patch over here today"; say, "you coming with us?" She say, "No, no thanks. I don't feel like going today." And she didn't go. She wasn't no young woman and she had to rest up after getting hit that night. And so, then Momma and them got some newspaper and put some newspapers down there by the bed, and Poppa decided that he would plan to catch her. He waited till she came, and she did, about two or three nights later. Pa got right out the bed, he said, and got his cord and reached to tie her up. The thing jumped from Momma and jumped across that bed and Pa tried to catch it but he couldn't catch it. So afterwards he sent Momma on down to Dawson to get some rest.

Pa and them used to say that the spirits of the dead most always visit back to the places where they passed away, and I believe that they do come back sometimes. When I first moved into the house I'm in now, I used to sleep in the front room on account it was easy to get to the telephone there in case somebody called. I had a couch in there that used to open down into a bed. One night I was asleep there and in my sleep it appeared that somebody was sitting on my pillow. I don't like for anybody to sit on my pillow, period. So I pushed myself back. I pushed myself back so hard I woke myself. And he spoke so plain I could hear it all in the house, "You don't know who this is sitting here." It kind of scared me. It shook me so until I was scared to go to bed the next night. That voice spoke all over the whole room. But I prayed it off. I never tried to find out who he was, either.

After that happened, I was sitting in the bathroom one day and had the door opened. The door across the hallway to the dining room was opened too and my great-grandson—a little bitty boy about two years old or better—he was playing out there and I could just see him playing and laughing like there was somebody in there with him. I looked at him; I looked in front of him. I didn't see anybody. Then he got up and started to the door going from the dining room to the front room. The door opened and when he got right up to it, it shut. He looked at the door; he looked up there and I called to him not to go out of the dining room. He looked at me, and then he went on back to playing. I walked the floor then and I talked to whoever it was. I didn't see anybody, but I told them I was there to stay, and I wanted to stay there. I didn't want to be scared, and besides, I said, "I wouldn't do you like that." I talked to whoever it was, and I ain't been worried that way since. But I wonder about things like that sometimes.

When someone died people used to sit up. They'd have a sitting-up all night praying and singing. I never heard my people say they were praying them in—you know what I mean. If they ain't got it, they won't get it. We didn't try to give it to them afterwards. They sang and prayed with one another, that's all. 'Cause God knows, if he ain't already got it, that's it. That's all of that. And you know, I remember in Miami—and also I heard of it in Milan, Georgia—a man was declared dead and he come back. You know now, if he had fell to that undertaker he would have killed him sure enough. Mr. Jim, one of my stepfathers, saw that. He was real scared of dead peoples. I mean he was a good man; my mother married him and I know what I'm talking about. That man, he would wait on you; he would give you his last. But you die, you shut your eyes, and he was through with you. I ain't joking. Well anyway, he was at this sitting one night, and this boy came back. My stepfather had marks on his leg where he jumped and was running, 'cause he got scared when the boy raised up there and the barbed-wire cut him as he was flying to get home. They were all running. He was in front, and a lady named Miss Sue, she say when he jumped that fence, Miss Sadie grabbed his coat. She wasn't gonna let him leave her! She liked to broke his leg. But anyhow, a lot of people were running. That happened right in Milan, Georgia. It's true. It was really something. Now the boy didn't know what they were running for, didn't know what it was all about, what was the matter with the people. They just tore down and ran, folks hollering all outside. After a while, somebody went in there where he was and talked with him. So that's why I say a lot of them ain't dead now when they take them in, 'cause sometimes they just go in that way and folks say, ah, she dead, she dead. She might be in a trance sometimes, we don't know. When my momma died, Mr. Julius, he say they gonna wait sure enough a long time before the doctor carried her away from there. He say they gonna sure enough wait.

People decorated the graves back then if they wanted to. Sometimes the dead person had a habit of certain things they liked to eat out of or certain things they liked to drink out of or a picture they liked—they put them on the graves. I don't know what they put them there for—to entertain, I guess. I don't know. And they'd punch holes in the bottom of the glasses and such—maybe to keep out snakes and other things from settling there. I put flowers on my mother's grave. But when you do a thing like that, be sure you put a hole in what ever you have the flowers in. Yes sir.

And they had many different signs about what to do around the dead. Like Mr. James, he was real scared of dead people. So they told him, say, that all you had to do was take the dead person's hand and rub it over your face and so you won't be scared of them no more. "Shoot," he say, "Oh no! I ain't gonna do that." They carried him up to a place one time where he was going to be made into the Lodge and that man run, you hear! They had a dead body up there and they had to run and catch Jim to carry him back there to finish making him. Jim didn't want to be no more Mason. He wasn't joking about being scared, either. My momma was then what you call a sick-committee person among women that specialized in the church, and when anybody die, she'd be one of them that would help watch with the people, and she was real good at that. Now anybody could come to our door and hail for anything, but if they come there for a death, Mr. James ain't seeing them and don't know them. A lot of people laughed at him because he was so scared of the dead, but he was the cutest thing. That man was a good man too, if you hear me.

The old people used to know all kinds of signs, and they had powers, too. They knew signs, like what the itching of the palm meant—and it's not the same for everybody—or the itching of the nose. You got to watch these things about yourself and learn to tell what they mean for you. Some old people used to take a sign from their ears burning. When your ears burned, that meant somebody was talking about you and you're supposed to rub it and say, "If you're talking good, talk on; if you're talking bad, please stop." And if the burning stops immediately that means they must've been talking bad. If they keep on talking, they must be talking good. And they had the nose-itching sign too—and that one works for me. If my nose itches on the end, that means somebody is coming riding; if it's itching way up at the top, that means they're coming walking. Or if they aren't actually coming they're talking about it or got their mind on it.

When you're going somewhere and the screech owl quivers on the lefthand side of you, they said it was a sign of death. A woman's death. When the screech owl was on the righthand side of you, then it was a man's death. And if the owl came into the house, you knew there was going to be a death there, or else you were going to move. Either way you were getting out of there. Some people say the fire or the light draws the owl inside, but he knows that ain't no tree when he comes in.

The old people had those signs and we learned about them. But there were other things they knew about living as well, that some was passed down and some weren't, like using herbs and plants, and just knowing the way of things around you. My grandfather used to be able to talk to a table. It had to be a diamond table with five legs. But he'd take his little finger and put it in the middle of that table and say something—I don't know what—and that table's leg would bump. He never did teach me how to do that.

And he could go about wherever he wanted. If he came up on a bad dog, I don't care how bad a dog it was, he could make that dog shut up. He'd look right at it and that dog wouldn't even bark. There's a passage in the Bible that says, "Not a dog shall rule this child." I know where the word is, but I don't know how to handle that one. Poppa could do it. All of them could do it. They understood how to hold the attention of the animals and things around them.

And times where we were going down through the woods to go fishing, they'd know where the rattlesnakes were bad. Pa would go first and it would be alright. No need to worry about rattlesnakes for the rest of the day. I knew they used to catch rattlesnakes with silk, but other than that, I don't know how they conquered them. To get them with silk what you'd do is tie a piece of real silk—we had real silk back then—onto a stick like a fishing pole, and once you knew where the rattlesnake was, you'd drop that silk on over there. You ease it on over there so he can't hear it. Then you chunk a rock or anything and the jarring will make him rattle and start getting into his coil and looking at everything that comes there. He's gonna stay there and you let him stay until he gets into his coil. Then you move the silk. When you move it, he hits it. When he hit, he can't get out of it. You see, when he hits, he has to turn over to get that poison out, but when he turns and he's in that silk and it's in his teeth, then he can't even bite himself. See, a rattlesnake will bite himself if he sees you're gonna kill him. He'll bite himself sure enough and poison his meat, his hide, everything. None of it's any good any more because of that poison. And so Pa and them would catch him that way in that silk. I saw them do that several times. Then they'd skin him like you would an eel and get that oil from where a gold-looking yellow streak is on both sides of his tail—that's the real rattlesnake oil. It makes liniment. And they'd tell us when we went into the woods to hunt huckleberries and pick up berries or anything, to do like the Indians taught them—break a green bush and stick it in your belt. Snakes would get away from you.

Then there's nettleweed—it keeps you built up, and it takes worms and stones out of you. That's the same common little thing called stinger nettle or bull nettle. It'll sting if you walk and touch it any old way, but if you hold your breath and touch it, it won't sting you. Just don't breathe if you're gonna touch it. That's how folks used to do years back, my grandfather said, when they broke the chain gang. They'd just come right through the stinger nettle so the dogs couldn't trail them. God gave us wisdom for something and they had to study well, those people who got put on chain gangs for nothing. That ain't no joke. But that nettle is good for more than one thing—it'll build you up, it'll help you.

Passion weed is something I used to play with as a child, but that's the best stuff to use for your nerves. It used to be plentiful on St. Simons, but now they've done built so many houses you can't find it. We used to play with the little fruit off it in my grandfather's time and we called it maypop. We'd chunk them when they were green, and you had to catch them right else they "may pop." We'd call, "Heel over, may pop!" to let you know you shouldn't grab it, cause if you grab it too hard, you may pop it. Some children used to eat the little melon when it got yellow ripe, but I never did because it smelled too high.

The way I know for people to learn to read the signs is simple. You have to watch them, pay attention, and see what happens. Like when your hand itches you, some folks pay it no mind but there's a sign in it. My left hand is letters, my right hand is money. You watch yours. Momma used to tell me one thing about it, she said, "Your right hand is money but don't think you're gonna have it all the time." You're gonna handle it but it may just pass through your hand; that's true. Sometimes when people are writing checks I can just tell that somebody's fixing to load up the wagon. Somebody's fixing to send me something. Money in my hand. And we had a way of doing, say, "Rub it on wood and make it good," if you got any wood, you know. But I have other ways with mine. I kiss mine and say, "God the Father, Son, and Holy Ghost command it whatever we do."

Now one kind of sign I don't have is about water—to know things by the water. That wasn't for me, I suppose. I know how to watch the weather but I have no signs of water.

I do have a sign in my fingers, when I cut my nails. I got my own sign and I watch it. But folks know if you cut your nails off on a Monday, then you got to pay for it before the week's out some kind of favor. On a Tuesday you get a whelp. You hurt yourself somewhere and don't even remember how. On Wednesday you get a letter or something better, and it would be a favor or something like that. On Thursday a new pair of shoes. Ain't that good! You're gonna get something new, that's all. And on Friday, that's unknown sorrows. That's when you sit down worrying about something but can't remember what it is. Something on your mind; you're burdened and you're sorry about something but you just don't know what it is. And they say if you cut your fingernails off on a Saturday that you'll see truly of the morrow, but as sure as you cut them off on a Sunday, the devil gonna rule you all week. You'll be snappy and can't be satisfied the whole entire week. Now that really works for me, it does.

Then there's a whole lot of sickness that comes in different ways, like sometimes you sleep depressed or sometimes folks meet you with a certain word and you can hardly take it. You feel it right in your stomach and you're snapping right back. You have no thought before you speak, 'cause you can't be bothered. Every little scratch or pain that comes along looks like it cleaves to you, hurts you in your bones or whatnot. There are many diseases and things like that you could keep off of you if you wear your underclothes next to your skin turned the wrong side out. It's a common thing. But if you remember reading that Jesus never wore a raw seam, you see where you should turn it out. And say, "Lord take away all sickness, all madness, those I meet and those that meet me, and teach me how to meet people; speak for me, Jesus," then put them on. And it'll be much better your whole entire life. I just don't wear no pants no other way but on the wrong side, and sometimes I find myself putting on my slip on the wrong side. I know I got to meet the best and I got to meet it with a smile. They may be hard but I know how to meet them. All that evil is cut out; it's gone. Like my grandfather when he'd be going along and see a spirit, he'd take off his hat and turn it wrong side out; he'd turn his pockets wrong side out, then he'd go backwards. See, all those things were signs; they were just little old nothings, but just as real as I'm sitting in this chair. I've continued with it and it continues to do me good. At least it ain't done me no harm.

I took a job with a white lady one time, and people said they knew I wasn't gonna stay there long 'cause couldn't anybody st\y at that place. They allowed me two or three days. I worked there close to two years. They wanted to know, "How could you stand old lady Gray there?" But I just went in there with a witness— Jesus. See, he made her just like he did me. See, she had a habit, a voice, and her talk was rough and abrupt with everybody whether she was on the phone, or at table, whether she was talking to her children or to me, and people didn't want to worry with it. And one little girl said, "You know why Grandma talks so independent? Cause she's so rich." I said, "She just talks like that, that's all." People just naturally didn't like the way she talked, but it was only talk and she wasn't making anybody do anything.

Her little grandchild went to the Frigidaire one day—the girl didn't know what she was doing—and stuck her finger in a watermelon. So the old lady came in, "Who stuck their finger in that watermelon?" The child said, "Bessie must've don it. That was Bessie." I went in there, "What're you talking about? What is this?" The old lady, "Nothing, she's telling a lie 'cause you ain't got no finger like that. Put your finger in that watermelon, gal." And the little girl's finger fit right in there. She tore her up, you hear me! Then after that I heard her in there talking with the child's mother about how the girl would be a liar and destroy people. See, that's just the way she was, that's all. You have to meet a person and find them out. People used to be surprised when the man who worked with her—his name was James and he had a truck and used to do hauling—would come to the house with things she'd given to me. Nice things: rugs, chairs, and bagloads of other things. But it wasn't anything special to me.

People sometimes want work; they need it and would work if they could get a job. I could help a lot of folks here in town that way—I mean streetwalkers and such, women or men—but they don't want it. And you're not supposed to give that which is holy unto a dog. Anything that you have good and really righteous, you don't give it to just anybody out there who cares nothing about it, ain't studying you, and don't have any appreciation. Don't give anything holy unto the dog; that's what the Bible says. But sometimes when it seems you can't hardly get a job, can't hardly stay on a job even after you've done the best work you can because the evil spirit or whatever is in your way, then read the Fourth Psalm. Read that psalm and if you're out of a job, you can get a good job. Not only that, after you get that job, then you continue to read it and you'll have more work then you'll be able to do. And that's the truth. God's got everything in there for us. It ain't hidden: it's true and it's not there just for certain ones but for the ones that need it.

I was helped with that in a church. This preacher was standing up in the pulpit telling the people, "If y'all want a job, those who want one, take this reader and read the Fourth Psalm. It's an old law—

> Answer me when I call, O God of my righteousness;
> Thou hast set me at large when I was in distress!

You're in distress when you ain't got no work to do and you can't do nothing. And it goes on to say,

> Son of man, how long will you turn my glory into shame?

That's when somebody is trying to kick you down, you see, and don't want to see you climb. Say,

> How long will you seek for less?

You see, seeking for the lesser things about me all the time, wanting to see me down all the time. Say,

> Know ye that the Lord hath set apart for himself
> him that is godly.

> The Lord will hear when I call upon him.
> Stand in awe and sin not:
> Commune with your own heart upon your bed
>     and be still.
> Offer the sacrifices of righteousness
> And put your trust in the Lord.

And he goes on to say there will be many

that will say, who will show us any good?

and say,

> Lord, lift up the light of thy countenance upon us
> For I have the gladness in my heart
> From the time that thy corn and thy wine increased.

And you know that's God's corn when it has increased, when the wine has increased. And you want that gladness in your heart, all the time.

Sometimes you'll find folks who have all kinds of strange signs, but it ain't nothing but foolishness. Like, they used to spit in the fire and if your spit dried up fast they said that was a sign you were going to die. Nothing but foolishness. Old folks had all kinds of junk like that. But now, the nose itch, that's a sign with me. Different people do have all kinds of different signs. Some people say if you go to sit in a chair and miss, then you ain't gonna marry. You'll never marry. But that's not true. I don't believe that. You just missed the chair, and maybe wanted to say something about it.

Yet people, no matter who you are, the spirits are around us all the time. Especially the old ones that know us and have gone on before—the ancestors. And we have the plants and animals that would do our bidding if we'd learn how to get through to them, plus the signs that tell us everything we need to know about what's going on around us. You have to be tried, and you're gonna be tried—it says so in the Bible. But most times people bring hardship on theirselves by not paying attention to what they ought to be studying and following behind what they ain't supposed to. It don't take much to know what's right and what ain't. If you want to know, you can learn sure enough.

See, the Lord warns some people. Fact is, I believe He warns everybody but they don't pay it any mind. I heard a woman once crying at her sister's grave. She said, "Lord, you showed me this but I didn't know what it was." God does show people things, but most of the time they just figure there's nothing to it. A lot of times the warning would be about you yourself. You know, when a woodpecker pecks on your house you're supposed to give it up, baby. Somebody close to you is going, or it may be you. That woodpecker, I know him. He done it to me. You got to look out for him because there's trees for him to peck on and he don't get no sap out of a house. He's a true sign. A lot of these things are natural truth. All the way down through the Bible it says, "These signs shall follow you." And some people can read signs so well until they can look at things and see beyond, and look at people and see things about them.

# 5

# Sea and Lightning

I REMEMBER the first little job I had out from home—I was around nine years old—and that was tending a white lady's baby. The baby was so large that I could hardly lift it in the crib and out. He was really heavy. But I was getting him in that carriage—they used to have them great big carriages in those days—and I was bringing him to home. It was a mile to my momma's house from where I was tending at: up them hills and down some hills. I remember he was so heavy I would just hold that handle on the back of the carriage and let him go on down and just follow, then carry him on to the house with Momma and them. And some of the children would go back with me sometimes to help me push him. This was in a little place called Herod near Dawson where I was tending that little baby at. The white lady would come and get me in the morning and bring me back in the evening, like that. But I loved tending little babies. And I've been tending children ever since I could do it.

And I remember one day a lady said to me, said when I got up to size I would hate children and I never would have any of my own. That hurt me real bad when she said that 'cause I used to play with folks' children all the time, and just loved to wrestle with them whether I could throw them or not, or to carry them whether they were big and fat or whatnot.

And so that day when that lady said I wouldn't have any, that sure worried me. Of course I didn't know about having children but I wanted children. She said it 'cause I loved them so well then, I guess. That's what she saw. But it was just part of me to want children. And I've often thought about it since then. She didn't know what she was talking about. And I used to wonder after I got on up why did I love children so much!

Poppa died in 1911, and right after his death we left Dawson. I can't think of the month, but it must have been the early part of the year, and it wasn't long after he died that we came on down to Fitzgerald with some more friends we knowed. You could make more money down there, plus Momma didn't want to be around Dawson. She just didn't want to be around there. So that's when we come down to Fitzgerald. I was out of school then, and Momma took a job at a place about nine miles outside town called Osierfield. Momma didn't say nothing about it, but I had worriation on my mind how we were going to make it. The white folks and them there had plenty of smoked meat and everything, but we didn't have it. And when we first got there I didn't understand that way of buying groceries, 'cause there wasn't no more farming, no more raising meat like Poppa and them did, but coming home with a bag in your hands. I thought I was going to get hungry and die. We never did do like that. When we had to get goods that way, it was kind of a puzzle to me and I didn't understand it, 'cause we'd gotten food in large quantities all the time. I was used to us having our own corn, and you'd go out there and shell your corn and carry it to the mill. We had our grits made, too—course they were coarser than the grits are now, but they were good fresh grits. See, one part of the corn make grits and one part make meal. We ground our own.

And too, Poppa had a way of getting by in Dawson. He worked with big farmers, and if he worked and saw where he needed some money and didn't get it, he'd mortgage those people's things and get him some money. And they never put him in jail for it. He mortgaged the white man's cow, pigs, and they wouldn't say a word about it. One time he mortgaged a sow with six pigs, and by the time they got out there to get the animals back the pigs were just on weaning. Sometimes they'd pay their mortgage, sometimes they'd just leave the animals there, but they never said a thing to him because he was a big farmer, a great worker, too. Another time he mortgaged a spotted milk cow named Bell—the cow and the calf—and it cost seventy-five dollars to get Bell back. I don't know how much the pig cost. But when he mortgaged Grandma's machine, that was a different matter. He didn't get off with that. When the man came to the house she said, "Oh, no!" She was a big woman, too, and she went out there with her apron on, "What you mean? Who mortgaged my machine? Noooo! You give me my machine back. You better get on back; you ain't getting my machine." She went down to the lot and told Mr. Greene about it and Mr. Greene paid the mortgage off. But that was Poppa. He'd mortgage it as sure as you're born; and ain't a thing ever happened to him.

But they were some good people out in Osierfield—I call them good people for those days—and we worked there and made pretty well. We done pretty well there. We stayed there a long time, and it was just Momma and me there for a while, but Momma later on married again. Momma married again, and again. She married five times. My momma married all her husbands— that was Jet, Jasper, Mr. Jim, Mr. James London, and Mr. Julius—and one day I said to Momma, "Momma, how come all your husbands' names start with a *J*?" I wondered that. She say, " 'Cause I didn't marry nothing but jackasses." That was so funny, I just laughed. Yeah, we had some time in our lives. But I never did like the marrying bit. Didn't like it from the beginning. I didn't never want to marry. When they were talking about me marrying my baby's daddy—no sir! I'll never forget that day. I just run around that house and I beat the walls to the house and to the chicken yard; I didn't like that junk—talking about being married. And he say, "Go on, let her alone. After the baby's born, she'll be okay." See, I never courted. I left school when I was about eleven and my baby born when I was twelve years old. But my baby's daddy was a grown man. I never did court, couldn't stand it myself. And I don't think I done wrong 'cause I yet can't stand it. I don't wish for nothing. But the mannish little boys—

they smell like roaches, you know—I couldn't be bothered with them things. I couldn't stand it and I just never did. Them boys be your age and everything but they act so funny! They try to be bossy, you know, and all like that. I've seen boys take a bunch of that santa spray—some folks call it cockspur—and hit the girls in the hair with those little stickers. That stuff get all in their hair and them boys think they done something big. But I always believed if he stick that in my hair, I'm going to hurt him. I'm going to hurt him bad. So that way I never did mess with boys. Never did. I was just comfortable without them.

My baby's daddy, he came up to Osierfield from St. Simons with some others when they had a strike down here. We had never heard about St. Simons, didn't know of any such place as this. But people on strike, they go to different parts of the country hunting work, so that their crew came up there. There were about twenty head of them, and about seven of them came there on the farm where we were. They had never picked cotton or nothing like that. They were fishermen and boat loaders. And they came up there. Course they knowed about cotton, but they had never picked none. When they got up in size enough to know, the cotton on St. Simons was already gone. Wasn't enough to make no living off, anyway. Anyhow, they come up there and so that's how I got in touch with him. I didn't know about nothing but that's where I got my baby. I didn't know what it was. But he was a grown man and he understood.

When they went down to work at a place called Hoboken, working for the same man, he must've known I was that way 'cause he wrote and told Momma that I was pregnant with his child. Sure did. Now you know them boys wouldn't have done that. Them old boys wouldn't have owned it. And so when the crew got back to Osierfield, they come talking about marrying. I ran around that house and hollered, "Don't you do that! No, no no." They had an old song, go "The man I'm going to marry ain't never been born" or something like that, and I would get that song, I would get it right away, and that's what I used to tell them: the man I'm going to marry ain't never been born. He knew I was serious, so he told them to let me alone. That was

1914. I was born in 1902. See what I mean? Yes sir, I was twelve years old.

The first fish I ever caught in my life was a turtle, and that's while I was pregnant. Momma and Lil were up to the white folks' house washing. We used to work—wash and iron—for the white folks. They were up there washing and I went down to the pond—there was a big old pond right where we stayed—thinking to catch a mess of red-eyes, them little bitty fishes, for Momma and them. I threw that hook out there right under a little old tree, and when I pulled there comes this turtle, his long neck all stretched out like. It wasn't so big, but when I tried to get him off the hook I couldn't get him off, and I carried him straight up the hill right on to the house like that, and right on to the porch. He was swinging backwards and forwards and it wasn't my baby I was worried about so much as I was scared of that thing. I got him up there and I hung the pole on the side of the house straight up and he was still on there. He was on there hanging, flopping against the house, and I went up to where Momma was and stood there looking at her because they'd told me not to go down there on that dam—it was a long dam sitting down there—to fish.

Momma said, "What's the matter with you?" I say, "Nothing." So I sat on down there on the wash bench. Then Lil, "What's the matter? Have anybody been down there to the house?" Momma'd had to run an old white man away from down there one day and she thought maybe he'd been down there bothering me again. "Anybody been down to the house?" "No." So Momma say, "What ails you?" She had a habit of saying "fool." "What's the matter with you, fool?" "Momma," I say, "that thing on that hook." "On what hook?" she say. "What's on that hook?" I say, "I don't know. He got a long neck and he got a heap of hands." Lil say, "You been fishing?" I say, "Yeah. And he's on the hook." So Momma went down there to the house and there he was: turtle up side the house. Momma said, "Go on in the house. I'll get him off the hook." She didn't want me to see her take him off the hook and kill him since I was with the baby. And as I was turning away I heard her say, "I expect that fool done lost that baby." I'd brought that turtle all the way from the pond on the

89

hook but I hadn't bothered him. And that was the first fish I'd ever caught in my life.

But I didn't much want to eat none of him, 'cause I was scared of him. But Momma and them cooked turtles in those days and Momma used to cook a turtle by stewing it in green onions. Wasn't nothing to cook but the legs, and sometimes they'd cook that underbreast after they had cleaned it. A turtle ain't nothing much but leg inside, and Momma used to cook them same way she cooked gophers and such. She'd boil them after she cut all the toes off, and get all that black off, then she'd pot-boil them, get that wildish musk out of the meat. Then she'd use a little flour—or meal if we didn't have flour—and fry it. She'd let it get about done, good, then add a little warm water and green onions and let it smother. It's really good then. Alright. After Momma cook that turtle, I used to have a habit of going in there to steal a piece of it. Ain't nothing to steal but a piece of foot, but I wasn't thinking about that. I'm going up to the top of the foot, you know, get me a little piece off. So one day, Momma had a long dish of it up at the table after I done stole about twice. I got to the table to eat and I reached my fork to get me a piece out and every time I go in there I get a foot. I say, "Everytime I go in here I git nothing but foot." She say, "Uh, huh. I know now where my turtle was going." I told on my own self. I didn't say nothing, I just laughed, because I had ate it. And they must have been missing that meat.

My baby girl was born September 15th, 1914. My mother was bringing me up by herself then. I didn't have no daddy. If I'd had a daddy I wouldn't have had that baby. But when the baby was four months, Cassius—he was the baby's daddy—he and me we got married in Fitzgerald. John Davis, who used to sing with the Georgia Sea Island Singers, was brother to Cassius's father.

Well, like everybody else I went on back to work after the baby. Momma couldn't make enough alone and we needed the money, so I went back to work in the fields. I kept my baby in the field where I went to work. All of us carried our babies out there in a box or a tub, and put them under a tree in the shade somewhere. Later on down in Florida during the thirties and forties, when folks were picking beans, I saw lots of them carrying their babies. Sometimes they had a tub on their heads with their babies in there, especially the folks from across the sea— they knew how to do that. And if it wasn't a box or a tub, somebody was toting the baby to get where they were going, then they'd put it down and fix a canopy over it for shade so the baby would go to sleep. You'd carry your baby food and everything, too. Me, I nursed my baby and so I had the milk with me. But there were more babies in the field besides mine.

When Cassius first married to me up there in Fitzgerald, his family wanted to know was his wife black or yellow. I read that letter. His sister Mary Green wrote that letter wanting to know whether Bessie was black or yellow. They wanted to know, because they say that the up-country women, the yellow women, would come to the coast and act bossy, and they didn't like the yellow women. And so I was glad I wasn't a yellow woman at that time because I would have felt bad myself. And I said to Cassius that those colored people ought to be ashamed of themselves, 'cause all my cousins were yellow and he was near about yellow. He knew better but they didn't know any better. That was their way.

I first came down to the coast in the year 1919 to a funeral. Cassius's baby sister had died from influenza and we came down to the funeral. And that day when me and Cassius and his sisters got on the boat from Brunswick to St. Simons, we were standing there talking to different people and Mary made acquaintance with me. She looked at the baby, turned the baby this way, turned her that way, alright. After a while she said, "Come on, let's sit down." I didn't know where Hatchet—that was Cassius's nickname—was, so we went and sat down. I was thinking that we were still in the depot. It was just like sitting down in a train depot. After a while she says, "I wonder did Hatchet get on board? I haven't seen him yet." And another lady standing at the window said, "It's been twelve years since I've been on this boat." I say, "Oh God!" I didn't know I was riding. I hadn't felt a thing. But I looked out there and it was nothing but water. I had to look back to see where the town was. That was something! Then she

91

said, "Come on, let's go out on the patio"—she called it a patio and that's what it is, you know—and we went out there on the deck and there was Cassius and some others. They all had parasols and he was out there having fun. I didn't stay out there too long though, because I was scared. I was just scared, that's all. I'd never been on the water before.

And just about that time the man on the boat yelled, "Hold fast! We broke down!" Lord, I thought I was going to die. But the Atlantic boat was going by and they beckoned her. That Atlantic boat came up close aside and some men got off and went down to the boiler room or somewhere down in there, and they did something and we went on. By the time I got off at the dock in St. Simons—where the pier is now—I knew I wouldn't want to go back.

When I got off that boat, the wind was high and that breeze took my hat off vroom! before I knew it. Anyway, one of the men who was already out there swimming just caught the hat and brought it on back to me. The dock had a big dance hall overhead and it was pretty. You'd have the lights up there at night and people dancing and going on. They'd carry us down there to see how it was. They had hacks running from the dock and they had a streetcar which would run from there to the different hotels and rooming houses. We had it: big dogs. And Willis Proctor, he used to run the hack with two big horses, and they'd come down and carry people to all sorts of places.

I ended up staying with Sarah Ramsay on the North End for about three months. It was a beautiful place and the people were very good to me. They were good all the way and they're still good to me. When I stayed over in Brunswick, I stayed with Mary, Cassius's sister who'd written the letter asking was I a yellow woman. The one that died, her daughter still lives on the island now and she's got some pretty children—four boys. She was a little girl when I first came down here.

I had never heard geechie people talk before—I call them geechies, but ain't no such thing as geechies—no more than Cassius and some of the boys he was with up there, but I had never been amongst so many, especially little children. Well, I love

children. And so when I came over here I used to get the little
children playing games. And with their games and mine, they
were right with me. They had the funniest sound I had ever heard
in my life when they talked, and I'd give them pennies—I'd go
and get a dollar's worth of pennies just to give them—to hear
them talk. Those children are grown people now, and two of
them done died these past few months, but they were children in
those days and they were something. I tell you. One had a little
speech she used to make—

> Look at my preetie leetle ruffle dress
> Look at my leetle locket
> I theenk myself a lettle woman now
> Because I have a pawket.

I thought that was the cutest thing. I'd give them money over
again just to hear her say that speech again.

As I said, we called them geechies, but there ain't so such
thing as a geechie. Nowhere. They call them geechie 'cause they're
salt-water people. But they came from across that sea just like
your foreparents or mine. If you stayed here a long time, stayed
down on the water, you ain't going to stay nowhere else but on
the water. 'Cause they get a better living. It makes better sense
than being up on that farmland following that mule around, you
see. You hardly get a salt-water person to stay in the midlands.
They like browsing around; they like to go out and catch them
some shrimp, or fishes or whatnot, and git that grits and things
and make their own meals if they want to. And when they work,
you pay them for what they do. That's all. They ain't fawning for
you. And the salt-water people—like from different parts of the
West Indies and them other countries over there—they're inde-
pendent-minded. 'Cause they come that way. And they call them
geechies 'cause they love the salt. They stay on the salt water;
others call them lowland geechies. But they're the same thing as
their ancestors from Africa or Haiti or Nassau or wherever. Yet
people got that word—"You geechie, you!" But it's funny, there
ain't no such thing as geechie.

There were some bad people on the coast in those days—

people who didn't take no hunching. There weren't many upland people here, but Brunswick was full of salt-water people. They came from the Bahama Islands, Barbados, and other places. There were lots of them here at that time and they'd cut you open, leave your body to bleed. So naturally that meant that times were a little different. Many of them were sailors who came over in boats and things. That's how my mother's last husband came over here. He said he worked on the water for twenty years, that's why he liked soup so much. He could have soup three or four times a day, and he had a time when he came over here. He didn't have any papers—he slipped off from the boat—and they had a time getting his papers. There was a man up at Frederica who went for him for two years before they finally got his papers straight.

On that first trip to the coast I stayed with Cassius's family and friends for three months, when I went back to Fitzgerald. Up there I could have stayed with Momma if I'd wanted to, but I didn't. I stayed in my own place. We were there up around Fitzgerald for a long while just making a living at picking cotton on different plantations. It weren't easy; and sometimes people we worked with were downright robbers. We stayed on a place once where we were kind of a boss for that man. We were the only Negroes on the place but we went and hired the hands. We hired colored and white if they needed to come over and pick cotton or hoe cotton. This man had two plantations. Well some of the boys we hired would be single boys and they'd stay in the cotton houses—the houses for people in cotton—or if we knew them pretty well, they could stay with us. Some of them stayed weeks at a time to pick cotton and help with cotton and all that stuff. This man had some cotton! His name was Wheelbright. He was a member of the grand jury and we stayed with him for almost eight years. So they used to leave the weighing scale at my house on the porch sometimes, and see, when they first buy them, those scales are already loaded with the proper weights. They're loaded from one to two pounds when you first buy them. So one day I looked at that scale and there was a whole hunk of lead—it looked like silver but was really lead like you'd melt off a bullet—near 'bout to the end of that pail. Nobody could hardly get two hundred pounds of cotton! I don't care how much they pick. That night I sat down and heated that thing on the fire until it got warm, then I took me some pliers and pulled that whole hunk out. It came out neat and even to that which was in there when it was bought. Just a whole hunk of lead. We went in that field the next day and we picked. And finally them sheets were coming up there: eighty-five, ninety something for the little children, and others were two hundred and ten; we had some that were three hundred. When I walked up there—I'll never forget it—he was saying, "Something must be the matter with them scales." I say, "No sir, ain't nothing the matter with them. I took that lead out that was in there!" Right in the field. He ain't said another word. And some of the Negroes didn't even know what I was talking about, but some of them did. One of them said, "Woman, ain't you scared?" "I ain't scared of nothing." He knew about that scale all that time he was picking cotton and never did open his mouth. I took that big hunk of lead out of there and I carried it with me for a long time. Yes sir.

I came back with the baby to Brunswick three or four times before Cassius died. Not to the Island, just to Brunswick. I used to stay right there on Amherst Street with Sister Mary. I'd ride the train to Brunswick, but I didn't go to the Island any more until I came back from Florida in 1933, because I wasn't roaring to ride no boat, you see. I could see the people from the Island when they came across. Cassius would come sometimes too, to see Mary when I didn't come. He'd come to see any of them if he wanted to, until he got sick. When he got real sick, then we all came to Brunswick, and then he died there. He died there at his sister's and we buried him on the Island. After Cassius was buried I left the coast with my girl and we went back to Fitzgerald. We stayed around there a good while. Then we left Fitzgerald and went to some other towns like Osierfield, until Momma went to Millen.

When Momma met "somebody from home, chile" and she decided to marry him, I was ready to move. His name was Jasper Johnson and he was her second husband. After they got married we moved from around Fitzgerald to Millen, Georgia. When we went there, it was about time for my daughter to go to school, and she went to school there until it was about time for her to go to the eighth grade.

Jasper Johnson turned out to be a dangerous man and he didn't last long in Millen. Momma then married Mr. Jim and went into renting out there. Mr. Jim was a good man. He was afraid of the dead but he was a good man.

Once I got sick off some fish I ate, and about six years before then he'd been kicked by a mule and the blood-poisoning done something to him, so years later his feet swole up and he was a sick man. He had to crawl across the floor. And I was sick in one room and he was in the other. We were living in one of them big old farm houses, and I remember Momma had to hire people to help her work her farm. And me, when I get to feeling too bad I'm going to get out of the bed. I'll just git down and you might find me somewhere on the floor because the bed gets too hot for me if I don't feel good. I prefer to lay on a pallet or somewhere.

Anyhow, when I go to get out of the bed, he'd be peeping across the hall. And if I had to go to the bathroom—we didn't have a bathroom, we had buckets—he'd crawl across the hall to my bed and put his shoulder against the bed and I'd climb out on his shoulder and he'd just lean over to the other side. Then we'd rest awhile until the time for me to go back, then he'd help me back into the bed. Now he was just that good. We were both down, and some people came in and out through the day bringing us lemon and water with chunks of ice—helping Momma with us—but he was that good and he couldn't walk. We both came down almost at the same time, I taken a little ahead of him. I ate some mudfish, which ain't so good of a fish, you know, when they muddled this pond where the water wasn't running. They got many fishes, and got many people sick, too. Because, see, there was malaria in that fish—that's why I took sick.

I was twenty-two years old and I had never been down sick before. I haven't been really down sick since, either. I've had a headache now and then, and my old age is following me now, but I never had a serious backache in spite of all the hard work. And I done some hard work. That was hard work that year—Momma had that great big old farm out there, the cotton was shiny! And that was in Millen, Georgia, up there near Augusta, about fifty-eight miles from Augusta. Yeah, I tell you, that was a sick time. I was sick enough that year not to be sick any more. Folks thought I was going out of my mind, I was so sick. It took me a few months to get better, and that was mostly because I took that doctor medicine and it liked to kill me. But after a while they got it out of me and had me drinking our own herbs and teas and things like that, until I got better. My stepfather's leg, they had to cut it open, finally, and the stuff in there was black like cold blood. And some of that stuff they say was from that old bruise when the mule kicked him six years before.

A mule will kill you and ain't no help for it! I was brought up around them buggers but I was scared of them. Momma wasn't scared of them. She used to try to break a mule, break him in to be a better worker, but I was afraid of them. Right now I got a big old scar mark where a mule ran away with us. We were in our wagon carrying corn to the mill, and my little girl, who was nine years old at the time, she was sitting on the corn. Momma and Mr. Jim were on that little old seat—we had a one-horse wagon, called a jersey wagon—and Miss Mamie, Momma's sister-in-law, was sitting in a chair in the back with me. The mule was named Susie and she started running away. They said she saw spirits and that made her run away. But anyway, there were other folks going to town, some in wagons, and Susie was passing them just like folks racing somebody. She was passing them and people were saying, "Look at that mule!" So we passed somebody's house and they hollered, "You know that mule runaway, Jim!" Mr. Jim say, "Let her go, she be alright." He had the line slacked, didn't have no tight line on her at all. She had her head bucked down and was just going. And just before she turned, Miss Mamie said, "Look at George!" By that time we were over.

And George, Susie used to be his mule until he got struck by lightning. He was dead. I ain't seen nobody. I didn't see nothing—but the ground. But what turned us over was an oak scrub that hit that front wheel and Susie went down to the ground and she trembled. That great big hunk of mule went down on that ground neighing. I hit that ground, wondering about my child. I said, "Oh Lord, where my child?" When I seen her she was up in the wagon—the wagon had tilted up on its side—holding the side of the body. "Here I is, Momma, here in the wagon." She was the only one didn't leave that wagon. Momma had fell, and Miss Mamie was way over there. It was a hilly place, and she fell tumbling on her head and it stove her neck down in around her shoulders somewhere.

Then Mr. Jim went and patted Susie and talked to her. He wasn't scared of her, but that mule was shaking just like somebody with a chill. That was in Mountain Grove Church graveyard, and people were just stopping and some of them were talking about it, and they were saying that Miss Mamie was going to have to go to a doctor. I figured I wasn't hurt. But folks carried us to town and we went on. They say, "You need to go to a doctor too." I say, "I don't need to go to a doctor. I ain't hurting." Then they say, "With all that blood on you?" I looked back, and my dress and all was full of blood. But I didn't even feel it. That little tin thing on the body of the wagon, that must've slit my thigh when I was going over. The cut wasn't too deep, but it was a long thing, and it didn't hurt. But, uh, uh, I don't want no mule.

Along about a week or so after that, Momma was in the white folks' house sweeping. I went up there and I spotted Momma. Then I got me a long stick and I didn't go in the lot, I went to the fence, and when Susie got near to me I hit her. She went to running—buggety, buggety, buggety—and I just hit her. Momma say, "What are you doing?" I was a big old grown woman, too, with a nine-year-old child, and I didn't want Momma to see me, but I was beating the devil out of that mule. I wasn't satisfied until I beat her some. Momma say, "Let that mule alone," but I beat her some.

See, where we were they used to order mules from Texas, and they called them wild mules. And different Negroes, and poor white crackers too, folks working on the farm there—it was a big plantation—each person would pick out one to break, and then that would be their mule to work with. And Susie was Mr. George's mule. After Mr. George got struck by lightning, then Mr. Jim took the mule down to his lot so we had two mules. At that time he was running what they call a two-horse farm, and he had another man to help him called Drake. So Drake had Ada, the other mule, and Mr. Jim had Susie.

Mr. George got struck by lightning on this mule coming in from work. See what God can do? The man got struck but the mule didn't get struck, but she was scared by the lightning. George fell off right there in Miss Mary Jane Septin's yard and Susie kept going. Miss Septin said they saw the great big ball of fire, the lightning, and George fell in the yard right by their well and the mule just went on.

I may not be scared of lightning, myself, but I am scared of the one that handles it. I'm scared of The Man that handles that lightning. When it's thundering and lightning, I don't have nothing else to do. I'm afraid of him. He says he's terrible and I believe him. But another thing that I'm scared of is a person who isn't scared of lightning; something wrong with him. Something deadly wrong with him. Course he just might be stupid. I used to work for some white folks who'd be at table during a storm and lightning just a-going on all in their glasses. They just sitting there eating and they ain't thinking or paying nothing no mind. I just sit there and look at them knowing they're crazy. There's something needs buttoning up somewhere. 'Cause that's a mighty Man up in that sky there.

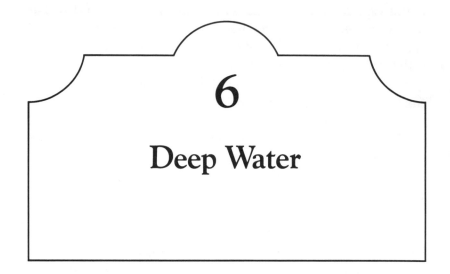

# 6

# Deep Water

IN THE DAYS when I was staying around Millen with Momma and them, I left once and went to Fitzgerald to visit. And there my cousin Clara Taylor and me, we got to talking with a friend named Ed Napa, who had worked down in Florida. Those were the days of the Florida boom, while at the same time there was less and less farm work around Millen. So Clara and me, in talking with Ed, we decided to go to Florida and find work. Five of us left to go together—Clara, me, Ed Napa, Horace Napa, and Charlie Napa. Horace and Charlie were brothers to Ed. That was in 1926.

When we got to Florida they were putting in a railroad down on the keys so Clara and me, we went down there and we found work washing and ironing for the workmen on Key Largo. I couldn't have handled it alone, but we worked together priming our own fresh water from the ground, and washing, and we did our own cooking ourselves. While I was down on Key Largo I picked up a game from the children there, "Way Down Yonder, Hey," and that's one of the games that I've kept up.

After a while we left the Keys and went back to Miami. We had a friend there named Wilbur Moore. We'd met him with the circus in Fitzgerald, but he wasn't working the circus any more, he was working on the railroad. He was a pullman porter. He found us a room and everything, and helped us in Miami, but the living there was too fast for me. Fast living everywhere. And so, with my mother on my mind, because she was back in Millen and I knew she was getting on, I was looking for a way to get back home. I didn't have hardly enough money, but I was "going home." And that day I was on the street, crowds of people everywhere; I mean people everywhere. And I was standing on this corner in the crowd waiting for the traffic to change so I could cross, and this man came up right there and offered me a job. All those people there, and he picked me out. His name was Bullard Jackson. He was a Nassau and he was working for some white people and looking for someone to do the cooking and be maid for the family and he picked me out. I went with him. The white family was from Tifton, Georgia, and the man was a plumber. I stayed with them a long time.

While I was working for these white folks in Miami, it came where I wanted to get back to Georgia and I didn't want to go without some extra money to give Momma, so I was thinking what to do. Then it came to me clear as anything one night in my sleep: a number that I should play. It had three figures in it. I woke up and I sat on the side of the bed and wondered about it, and didn't quite know what to do. It said I should play three dollars—I didn't have but ten—and I wondered who I could talk to about it but decided I wouldn't say anything to anybody. That day I got through with my work early and went over to the place where they played. I sat down there and I looked at my three dollars and I couldn't do it. Lord! Help me Jesus! I sat there and looked at my three dollars and I could not do it. I finally bet twenty cents. Two dimes. And while I was sitting there a man came in and paid fifty cents to play the identical numbers that had come to me and he won four hundred dollars. Now what would I have made if I'd bet my three dollars? But I couldn't do it, because it isn't for me to do those things. I just can't stand to see that money go and that's why I could never be a gambler. Not in that way. See, if I got a good little batch of money on me, I figure I've already gambled. I worked hard for it and I got it but that wasn't guaranteed. You could work for a man but there's no guarantee he's going to pay you. He could have been paying you ever so long; there's still no guarantee. Some flaw can come up. And then you ain't guaranteed that you're going to spend it. So anyhow you look at it, it's a gamble and that's the truth. And you're in a gamble for anything once you start it. A lot of folks gamble otherwise and say that's gambling—rolling dice, and playing cards, and all like that—but that just causes fights and evil and confusion. I think they ought to stop that.

And as for stealing, I think you got a rackety mind when you got a mind for stealing. I see and read and hear about it every day—some girl with a jumpsuit in her pocketbook; another one goes in those shoe places barefooted and comes out with a brand new pair of shoes—it's terrible. Some folks say it's alright for black people to steal from white people. Black people don't have to steal from them white people. They take, in that way, 'cause they hardly ever get enough to say that they got anything. They just take something, that's all. 'Cause when you steal something and you can really live on it afterwards, then you got something. But that other little bit, that other little something, then you just get yourself in trouble. Like the little chillun go get chewing gum; they catch them with it they just as sure give them two years. And when they catch them with two or four hundred dollars, they give them two years. See, it's the same thing; they just got themselves in trouble. And when a colored person rob or steal from a white person, they're not taking nothing that was took from them. They just doing something their own self, 'cause they can't back that up. It's just way much too long, just too far back, and always have been and always will be. Always will be that they're gonna take from us. They're gonna cheat and steal from us some way. Like in business—they got the knowhow and they got the scales; they got all that in there.

Once while I was working in Miami, I was a cook, and the different cooks and maids, we had a day off. Thursday was our day off. Those of us who were friends together, we had a store downtown where we used to meet to buy different things. Some would be shopping for things to wear to church. I wasn't in any church then, but I liked to wear nice things. So this one particular day we had been buying and buying, and after a while I went into Kresges to look at their hats, because in those days I mostly wore hats. I went in there and I tried on hats, and tried on hats to see if I could find one I liked, and finally decided that I would let it alone. I wasn't going to get me one. I was going to leave it alone. So I went around that store and I bought me some Lonnie Johnson blues records—I picked them out and the lady played them for me and everything—and then Abe Sawyer came in there and I said, "Ooh, I'm going to see Abe Sawyer today!" and I went over there and saw him. He was a full-grown man but he was a midget. He was from Nassau and they said he was the richest man in Nassau. His wife was a tall lady, and when they were crossing the street in traffic she used to pick him up and put him under one arm. It would be funny with him kicking and saying, "Put me down! Put me down!" But she was a big old tall white woman, and though she had to get him unawares, once she picked him up there wasn't a thing he could do, and she'd just carry him along with no mind to his kicking and yelling. It was funny! It was always a wonder to me that they could be man and wife.

Anyway, I was walking along looking at Abe Sawyer until finally I got ready to go. All my friends had already left and I wasn't around anybody I knew, so I just went on and caught the streetcar—the Third Avenue streetcar. We went along until that car got between two tall buildings—the New York Department Store and the Firestone building—and that made it so you could see yourself in the glass. I looked around, and there I was with a tag hanging down my neck. Ooh, wee! And the hat! I could've fell out of that streetcar. There I was in the hat that I had tried on, and had left mine in there. I wanted to go backwards with that streetcar, and I could see every police in the world on the other end of that streetcar just picking me up. I didn't know what to do! And I didn't get off at my corner, either; I got off before that. The hat didn't cost but two dollars and twenty-five cents, but I felt chilly; I felt funny. And I didn't go back down there with that hat because you know they would've sworn that I meant it. It was no joke. But that was something, running around with those folks' hat on, while I was laughing at Abe Sawyer.

While I was in Miami I sent to Momma and got Rosalie, my daughter, and she went through school in Florida. She went to school more than I did, and schooled her boy and girl too. She didn't have but two children. She married a preacher in Connecticut and stayed up there over thirty years. That's where I got this fifth generation from; it's her children's children. Rosalie died about four years ago [1973] in Connecticut.

Down in Florida I met up with Sam Sebourne and I stayed with him a long time. He wasn't a husband or anything, but a good friend. I was going around with religion and everything and ended up with a man. Course I never could go with a man unless I liked him. I had to want him. And then, no matter how bad he wanted me, he had to do it again. Act like you want me; do it again. Try it again. That's right. I never wanted a man to think that I was so rushing for him. And all back then when me and my husband were together—and I had always heard this from the time I was little—don't care how angry I was at him I would always fix that man's food and his clothes. I would be so angry sometimes I wouldn't want to speak to him but I would fix his food and iron his clothes. When he came in to eat, I'd walk out of the house. I hear women say sometimes, "I ain't going to do nothing for that man." But that's not the way. You should do your part. You ain't got no excuse; you just do your part.

During 1928 me and Sam went down to the Gulf of Mexico; that was the same year they had a bad storm on Lake Okeechobee that killed a whole lot of people down there, and we had just about an inch decided not to go to the lake ourselves. There were five trucks of us left Miami going to look for work, and when we came to where the road divided—one branch going to the lake, the other way to the Gulf—we had to choose. Mr. Abbott, he was the oldest one with our bunch there, and he chose to go down to the Gulf, not the lake. There was a big work on the Gulf and we were to be cultivating. On the lake the work was mostly picking beans. Besides, the pay on the Gulf was good so Sam say he thought we'd do better on the Gulf, and I agreed. Three trucks of us went to the Gulf and two went to the lake. We never saw those who went to the lake again: they got drowned. Folks over there got drowned by the thousands, you know, they just got drowned in that storm.

But anyway, we went on to the Gulf, and got down there, and got to Marco Island. This was way down there on the Gulf of Mexico, ninety-one miles from Cuba. On one end of the island was a little town called Marco, and Goodland was on the other end. Our work there was to clear the land and cultivate this ground and make it one island and it's that way now. We did that work, and when you go there now it's one island. The two were six miles apart and they made them meet. The particular place where we worked from was a place named Caxambas. We met two Negroes there when we got there and they'd been there since 1922. The man was friendly but the woman mostly kept her distance.

So we went over there and we were doing that cultivating. I helped cultivate; I helped burn them palmettos: pile them high and set them on fire. My legs and things looked like I'd been whipped with stripes because of all the scratches from the bush. I had it bad. They dug up the palmetto roots and set them on fire too, and as long as they were burning we didn't get many mosquito bites. The mosquitoes were bad in that place. They would stop some jobs if there was no burning. People would sometimes have to put on masks, and the mosquitoes would cover those masks up. They were something, those mosquitoes down there. We had powder by the barrels to burn too, for the mosquitoes. You'd dip down with a scoop, dip it up, and burn that powder. Now you know those mosquitoes were bad: ooh! they were bad. There were plenty of mangoes and the mosquitoes were up in those trees. You'd go to the groves at night, and vroom! there come the mosquitoes. And so to sleep we had to cover with something, but the palmetto smoke would keep them off most the time.

And so we went down there, and we were burning those things, and I wasn't worried about the work until comes time to cook. I was the cook but I didn't have a sign of a stove. I was cooking for twenty-two men in between piling them palmetto bushes, and I had to cook for them without a stove. But you could do it if you try. I had three tin tubs, and I filled them up with dirt and rocks—dirt at the bottom and rocks at the top—and made my fire on top of that, and put my pots and pans on top there. And I cooked that way. I cooked bread, hoecakes, everything that way. I used to make hoecakes by the stacks for everybody. Then after a while, since we were expecting rain to come by the minute, the men built a tin shed all around my three tubs so I could be inside and it wouldn't rain on the fire. Then I had a table sitting there inside the shed and later they took a flue, a stovepipe, and cut a hole in the tin, and the smoke come right through that like a chimney. That flue would draw it. And we made it that way and made good money, too. We burned the palmetto branches to cook with.

The palmetto makes good coal when it gets down to coal so we burned that, and it was the best cut we had 'cause we had to continue burning it to keep the mosquitoes away. We also had that insect powder, the kind you used to buy in those little old cans called "B brands." Used to be, you go in a store and go to the insect section, you'd see the can with something look like a bee on it and they called it "B brand." But we got it by the barrels over there, that's right, 'cause mosquitoes were sure bad. Mosquitoes were something over there. But the palmetto smoke was good for keeping them away, so we had that too.

And those Negroes, the negro woman that was over there, she didn't fool with us. Therefore I didn't have nobody to talk to but just the men that were along working. The seaboat train used to run in there; it came in once a day and every time it come in and go back, they'd have to turn that track around to cross that water. See, nobody came in there unless they came in on a ferry or with them people. And so therefore it wasn't public. But the railroad was working over there and they had a railroad camp. The railroad camp people, they had a woman with them, and she too didn't have no women to be with way over there in that railroad camp. Finally I went over there and she was as glad to see me as

I was to see her. We became real friends. We'd have dinner to-gether. She and a few others would come over to our house and eat gophers. They would—I don't eat gophers. I cook them, but I don't eat them. But by me cooking for people, I got all sorts of things to cook—fish, gophers, 'gator tails, and all like that. I cook 'gator tails and the people just love that, you know. I never knew that people ate 'gator until I went down there. But they do. They clean them, and skin the 'gator for the hide, and people eat the tail. Mostly people don't know it, but many times you're eating seafood off your plate in some big restaurant and you're eating nothing but 'gator tails. They fix them in soups, too, and you get it in hotels and places like that. Yeah, 'gator tails; that's fish. Nothing but fish. But 'gator tails and gophers and like that, I never ate it. Cook it, but don't eat it.

Now fish, I didn't have to buy any of that. They had a clam factory there and I'd go down to the factory and tell them to save me some 'gator tails. See, they shipped them to hotels and places as a special meat but they gave to me 'cause we were there clean-ing up the place. That's the reason they gave to me. And that saved money. And my dog would go out and retrieve gophers like a dog trailing a rabbit. I'd hear him bark and go where he was at, and I've come home with five gophers or so many a time. They just cry, you know, the gophers do. They cries with tears in their eyes. But the way you catch them was, you'd have a long stick with an iron hook on it and you'd hook them before they dig down into their holes. Sometimes I'd reach down and catch 'em by the leg, but you got to be awful strong to get them that way 'cause they be holding on too. If you get the right hook on them then you got them, unless you can catch him before he get in that hole. That's what Jake would do. He'd try to keep the gopher from getting down in that hole. Jake was some dog, too! He was something.

Well, so anyway, we helped cover that whole ground up over there, and we made our little money. Sam had a big-six Stude-baker—don't hardly see them cars no more—and we thought we had something. I had never learned how to drive. Sam had wanted me to learn, and he tried to teach me, but even so I still hadn't learned well. So one day, after I had learned kind of how to drive, I said to myself, "I'm gon show him." I cooked and got everything out of the way and all, fixed my little kitchen and all the rest good. Everything was set. I say, "I'm going to show him I can drive. I'm going to the woods and get him." The day was kind of rainy-looking and I decided I'm going down there to the spot they were working at and get him. This is the Gulf of Mexico; we down in there. Now this ain't no joke. It's the deep blue water, you know. And I'm going to show him I can drive. I went in there and got that car. Alright.

The little shanty house I was in wasn't much bigger than a fair-sized room—just a shack. Wasn't no ceiling and we had hooks and nails on the boards inside to hang things like coats and clothes' we had a shelf for cups and things, then my pots and pans hang on the outside. Alright. I got in that car. Time I got in the car, old Jake—he was a big dog—he slips in the back like he would with Sam. He sits up there in the back looking. I started up the car, drove off and started to go around and I hit that house. I hit that house and Jake hit the floor. I hit it on the side, just enough on the corner. I don't know why, but I wasn't a bit scared. I didn't get panicky nor nothing like that. But I was trying to put on the brakes and was getting the gas at the same time. I knew how to stop it, but when I got on the gas and the brakes too that car was moaning "Aaa-wooh." That engine was going. And old Jake, he jumped up from back there, trying to see about me—he always sees, about me—until I finally got it cut off.

It was just lucky I didn't hit the stove, 'cause it was out there, and what I was trying to do was go around it and then come back out. I didn't drive over far enough and I hit the edge of the house and knocked over the blocks. The blocks had been little bitty blocks, and the door had been dragging funny and Sam had told me to call the man out there to come and fix it, and the man had been there and fixed it so it wasn't dragging any more. When I hit that house—the door was closed, you know—when I hit the house that made the door worse than it had been before the man came. What was I going to do? Sam would know I had his car.

Well, I got my hoe and shovel and I got busy. I took every block from under that house. I took every one out from under there. I got them all out and throwed them across the fence where nobody would see them, but from where I could burn them for wood later on. I got me a hoe, and I cleaned all around there. That yard was beautiful when I got through. I had it pretty. All back there where it was weedy there wasn't no more 'cause I cleaned them up.

I cleaned that place up and I mean I done it in a hurry, 'cause it wasn't too long before knocking-off time. I put that car back right exactly in the rut I got it out of. Alright. Sam and them come. Now the door was in a little bit worser shape and at first I couldn't get it to go back. But by me taking the blocks out, it did go back and so I had it already opened when he came. Later on that night when Sam tried to shut the door it dragged. He said, "My gee, the man ain't fixed the door? It ain't no better than it was." I said, "Sure ain't. He ain't done nothin' to it, just nothin'." Alright. The joist that we put our clothes on supposed to have been right over the bed, right there. But Sam ain't noticed that that joist was way back on the other side of the room. They didn't notice it. I was looking at it to see if they were going to see that that joist was twisted over, you see—the whole house was twisted—but they didn't notice that at all. Nobody noticed it. There was another boy staying there named Crip and we had a sheet between us and him—that was all betwixt us but it was a full sheet we had there, and clothes bags and things hanging to make a separation, so he could stay with us 'cause they treated him so bad down on the place. He was a cripple too, that's why we called him "Crip." He ain't paid no attention either. He smoked over there and he didn't even notice that the joist where he put his cigarette and things was moved. He ain't noticed. It was there, but ain't nobody noticed nothing. I said, "Thank you for helping me!" But so, by me pulling them blocks out that done a lot of good 'cause we couldn't have got in that house otherwise. Somebody would have seen, and I would have had to tell something.

We stayed there about another month 'cause the year was near about through, then we packed and went back to Miami. And you know, woman is the worse thing that God ever laid on earth if she ain't right. I can tell you about that too, 'cause I went through it myself. I was out there in the world before I married Mr. Jones; I call it in the bushes, 'cause you're just out there. Down in Florida Sam and I were staying on Sixth Avenue in Miami after we came back from the Gulf. He was a Nassau, and we were doing good. But there was something else over yonder: a guy who had a store and lived across the street from us. I was going with this guy too, when a lady came down from Savannah who knew him. She was all style, out of my boundary. I hadn't ever dealt with that kind before, but I wanted to make sure this lady saw she wasn't going to get anywhere with this guy. So one time Sam went up to the lake. He went to see how things were up there. He went to stay a week or two, then he was going to come back and we all were going to go up there quite naturally, if things were right.

Sam left, and I decided this guy—his name was Cecil—wasn't going nowhere that night but with me. So we were there, doing a little moonshining, and I was carrying on. I didn't want him to go no place, just stay there with me. I didn't want him going out with that lady. And he was trying to show me that he was just a friend to the lady, but you can't tell a fool nothing when he wants to be one. Well alright. I went on. I took his hat. He was walking around the room trying to talk to me, sitting on the side of the bed trying to tell me something, talk to me like he ought to, with good sense. "You ain't going nowhere," I said. "You're gonna stay right here." I was at Sam's house! But then, Sam was supposed to be up at the lake for two weeks before he came back. "You ain't going no place tonight." I took Cecil's hat and I threw it way up under the bed, then I dropped back and laid across the bed—and dropped off to sleep.

Cecil eased right on out and went on. He got his hat, too, but I didn't know that. He shut the door but he didn't lock it. He just shut it and went across to his porch. He laid up on his porch to look over at Sam's house, and watch to see if I didn't get up, because he knew he hadn't locked that door and if I didn't get up he was going to come over there and lock it. After a while, he said, a car came around the curve, drove in front of Sam's house and stopped. He looked over there to see who it was 'cause he knew he hadn't locked my door, and there it was—Sam. When I woke up Sam was standing over me at the bed. "My gee, Bessie, you git full of that stuff and lay there with the door open; somebody could come in here and kill you. My gee, git up from there. I want you to go over to my cousin's house with me."

I got up, one of the biggest fools you ever did see. I come sober. Low. I didn't know what in the world was happening. Where did Cecil go? Did Sam see him? He must've seen him. I said to myself, Cecil must be hid. I went to the bathroom first, 'cause I figured Cecil might have been in there. Sam couldn't have come in the back door because I had it locked. I made it to the bathroom, but wasn't nobody in there. And Sam seemed to be acting funny. Queer. He wanted to carry me to his cousin's house, and it came to mind he wanted to carry me there to kill me. He said, "Come on. I want you to go over there." Way over there about three miles away. One of his family was fixing to go back to Nassau and they were having a party or something. But what did he want me to go way over there for? I didn't know what to do. I washed my face with cold water. Then I acted like I was looking for my shoe and looked down under the bed to see if Cecil was under there. I didn't know what had happened to him.

So we went on to Sam's cousin's house. They had a lot of food cooked, but I said I wasn't going to eat any of it because I figured they were going to poison me. See! I'm in trouble. I done dirty. I'm low-down; I'm dirty. It says your sins will find you out and they were beating me to death. What happened? I was in bad shape. So we stayed there until near about day. Then Sam went off with the rest of the crew down to Fort Lauderdale about fifty-six miles. He still had work to do down there. Then they would be back. It wouldn't take them long to come back.

Back at Sam's house I went and got me a pillow and a quilt and laid it down in my door where the wind could hit me. I laid there with my head at the door. Then all of a sudden Cecil is

111

standing right there by me saying, "Read Proverb Seven," and he kept going. I didn't see that man any more for about eight or ten years. But I read that thing. I read that chapter in Proverbs until I couldn't hardly swallow that day. It just ate me up. Every woman ought to read that chapter in the Bible: "Let not thy heart decline to her ways and go not astray in her path. For she has cast down many wounded; many strong men have been slain by her; her house is the way to hell, going down to the chamber of death." It would have been that night too. It would have been if Cecil hadn't had good sense.

Now you think that's a bad woman! And they're still doing that, going along the street and swearing that they come to meet you. I wasn't on the street, I was at my own house; but yet and still, "Come over. You're going to stay here. You ain't going nowhere"—all them kind of old things. But it's death. It is death, that's all there is to it. Somebody had to have some sense. I never would: I was crazy. Say, Lord, will you forgive me? I'll never let this come up on my brains no more. I wasn't married to Sam but Sam was my delight. I went with Sam for four years and I never seen nothing with him. He never hurt me. What hurt me was what I'd done and he never knew it. Ooh! that was something.

But that defines a bad woman. They are bad. God tells you how they act and what they do. They come out, leave the good man at the house, and by speech and act cause other men to go astray. That causes death. Especially young men; they don't know no better. I think back on that temptation sometimes and I know I was blessed. That was foolishness, craziness, carelessness, that's all. I didn't have anything else to do. I had a good job and a good friend and he had a job—was no need of it. Just telling in your mind. It was just wrong. But I say thank God 'cause someone understood. The Lord was good to me. Now you take the last chapter of Proverbs and you get the good woman. The last chapter, beginning with the tenth verse. It's something, the way the Lord has blessed me to come out to be that same woman now: "A worthy woman who can find? For her price is far above rubies. The heart of her husband trusteth her, and he shall have no lack of gain. She doeth him good and not evil."

We stayed in Miami a good while, then went to work again. We went to the lake where they had the storm and all that killing had been—oh, it was terrible! So we went up there, quite naturally we were going back to farm. So one day I was telling it about knocking the house with his car. I told Sam about it and although that had done passed so long Sam said, "My gee, I thought something was wrong with my car wheels." I say, "That's just why I didn't tell you, 'cause I knew you were going to say your car was out of line." I had watched him. He came in that evening, and got in the car and went up to Caxambas to buy things from the store. I looked at the wheels to see if they were going to turn. Then he went off and turned, went his way and come back, and he didn't say a thing until we got way back to Miami where I told him, and "I thought something was wrong with my car wheels." I say, "Ain't a thing wrong with your car wheels." He say, "My gee, Bessie, you could've killed yourself!" And I could've, if I'd gone around and gotten out there with that car. But God stopped me right there, right there at the side of the house. Boy, I tell you, I went through something. Yeah, I was going to drive by myself.

And they had a habit of going fishing on a Sunday. I guess it's known long years ago they had a thing about Simon went to fish on a Sunday and the old folks tell you his belly busted and all like that. They told us all that and we believed it. We believed that it was not right to fish on Sunday, and quite naturally our parents didn't fish on Sunday, and we knew some folks didn't cook on Sunday. They would cook on Saturday nights and that's all. You don't get nothing else. We did cook on Sundays, but no washing, no ironing, and no scrubbing—no, nothing like that. And I was over in that part of the country then where everybody do everything on Sunday. And I thought they were the wickedest folks I had ever seen. So this particular day I didn't want to stay home by myself and Sam and them were going fishing. Course, where he come from over in Nassau, they fish on Sunday. And the folks up at the railroad, they wanted to go too. Everybody was going and I had nobody to stay with me. So they said, "Come on and go." And I say, "You know folks don't fish on Sunday."

"Oh, come on." I say, "I don't want no fish caught on a Sunday."
"Well, you ate a many of them already," they say, and so I decided
to go. I sure didn't like this fishing on Sunday, but I went on
down there.

Now this railroad track was over the Gulf, and where the men
used to go down to turn the tracks around, they call it a bridge.
They turn it around for the train to come over, and there was a
table down there where the train turn around. Well that's where
the men went, down that steep side, and they fished down there.
There was a little boy fishing up on the bank, and Sam told me
to stay up top with him 'cause down where they went was too
dangerous. Alright, I did. I was still worried while we were there
catching them fiddlers—little old things that look like crabs but
grow in the ground—to fish with. I was catching them little
fiddlers and I was afraid of them, but Sam baited my hook and
everything and left me some more fiddlers up there. So the little
boy and myself stayed there on the road and we fished. Finally,
after a while Sam hooked something down below. I could see it
'cause the sun was shining bright, and from looking down the
way I was I could see it quicker than him 'cause he was on the
same level as the water. And I'm scared 'cause the fishing on
Sunday, I don't like it. And he was holding that thing and it was
terrible. The way he was holding the line you could tell that thing
was pulling.

So I seen the thing and when that thing turned over I hollered,
"Turn him loose, turn him loose! You got a cow! You got a cow,
turn him loose!" I didn't know that it was a cow, yet he couldn't
get anything else but cow out of me 'cause I seen its ears and I
just knew that it looked like a cow. So I said, "Turn that thing
loose!" But it didn't look like no cow to Sam. In fact, it was a
stingray. A huge one, about as wide as a big bed and half as long.
One of the biggest ones I most ever seen. And by him flapping
them flaps of his in the water they look like the ears of a cow to
me. But they didn't pay me no mind. They pulled and pulled
until they pulled him in. That was the shiniest stinger! That
thing was just glittering away. And they put him on a plank and
cut the sting out and let him stay there. Course they could fish

off of him if they wanted to. Alright. I was still mad. I was still worrying. I said to Sam, "See what you got? See that thing there? I told you you shouldn't fish on Sunday." He say, "Awa Bess, go ahead on. Go on and fish, girl, fish. It ain't no sin to fish on Sunday." That was a stingray and I had heard talk of a stingray but I'd never seen one. Alright. They fished and fished.

After a while then I caught something. And by pulling the hook when it hit, I automatically forgot fishing on Sunday. I forgot it was a sin to fish on Sunday. I went to pulling that thing and I pulled and it was strong. They went to saying, "Hold it! Hold it!" 'cause they could catch the line better than I could and they brought it in. When they brought it in, that was a fish! He was a big one. And they brung him in down there. When I seen that fish I thought no more about this fishing on Sunday. They say, "Bring him on up there, bring him on up." I brought him on up, got him up there and then put him on the track. The boy said, "Wow! What a big fish!" Little white boy. I put my foot up on the fish then to take the hook out of its mouth, and it said, "A-HUM-DE-DUM-DUM; A-HUM-DE-HUMDE-HUM." That was a drumfish. And that's the way they sound when they're alive. But I didn't know it. I screamed, "Throw him back: he's talking! Throw him back! I told you you can't fish on Sunday!" I mean, I throwed him, too. And they caught him down there. "He's talking!" Course I'd never heard a fish say nothing. But he sound like a pure drum and that's why they call him a drumfish. You catch one, you catch you a live drum: DUM-DE-DUMDE-DUM . . . DUM-DUM-DUMDE. He beats it too, baby! And so that was a drum. I said "Throw him back, he's talking" 'cause I didn't know if he was going to say something to me like Simon, see. I started right then thinking about Simon and I never wanted to carry that fish home. But anyhow, they did. I throwed him in but they caught him down there. Oh yeah, he wasn't gon scare me no more. I mean, I had a time that Sunday. I stopped fishing right then.

And so, a little later on the little boy, he had something. I thought he had one of them things I had found 'cause that little boy was pulling so hard. He was up against that little old railroad tool house trying to hold it, trying to hold that line, and I held him. Then Sam and Mr. Dixon run up there and two other men came up, and they grabbed him 'cause they spied what was happening. They grabbed the line first and somebody say, "Uh, uh, son. Don't pull him in. Just hold it there. Let it stay in the water." It was an angelfish and they had seen it. And that angelfish, if he had gotten it above water it would have knocked him clean off that track. And they knew, 'cause they knew about fishing. They say, "Don't let him out of the water, baby. Let him stay in the water." See, as long as he stay in the water he could fight, but if that bugger had been pulled out then he'd spread, see, and come straight at you. That's what an angelfish would do for you. You have to know how to catch him. That long sprong on him, he line that up, and he'd come right to you and stick it in you and knock you out. And that being a little boy too, it would have hit him. And so they kept it in the water until they got out there and then they caught him. I said, "I told y'all it's a sin to fish on Sunday." There it was again. Ooh Lord, I declare, that was something. But that was a big fish. That was a big round thing that boy had. They brought him on home too.

I ain't never caught a drum since; the Lord fixed it. I fished all around there just as regular, Sundays and all like that, but never saw another drum.

Another day me and Sam went fishing. It was a weekday but there weren't no work and we weren't working. Sam and me, we went down there fishing. He caught a good nice mess of fish. Then sharks started coming up in the little sluices: the kind they call sand sharks. They were coming up where we caught the fishes at. Well anyhow, as we were leaving, I'm going to get behind. I had a good long rope, not too heavy, and I was going to show Sam that I was going to catch one of them sharks. You know, God has been good to me; it's good to see me here. I was going to show Sam while he was walking ahead of me that I was going to catch a shark and I wasn't going to call him until I had one. I had a piece of beef that I was carrying back home with me, about the size of the palm of my hand. Alright. I hooked that beef on two hooks, tied them on that rope. Now I'm going to tie that rope onto my wrist, you know, and then I'm going to throw it out, and I'm going to hold onto the railroad tracks with my other hand. Not knowing that that sucker could've pulled the arm out of me. I didn't know it. Sam looked back, God bless him, just as I was getting all set, and he say, "What're you fixing to do?" I say, "I'm going to catch a shark." The way my hand was, he seen the rope. He made it there and grabbed the rope, took his knife and he just cut it. When he cut it the bait hit the water, and when it hit it went zzipp! It was gone. The sharks had it. He say, "Bessie," he say, "come on. You go home. He'll kill you." I say, "That little old thing? I can pull him out." But really, after I seen that thing caught the beef like I did, I felt funny. I felt curious with myself and knew I wasn't going to try that no more. It was a dangerous trick.

Another dangerous trick I tried, right on that same track, was when I went down there fishing with Mr. Dixon and a girlfriend from camp, who said she was coming a little later on when she got through with her stuff down there. So I told her I'd be down on the track and I went down there, and so pretty soon here she come. I was fishing and something got my hook in the water and hung it beneath that table. There was a ladder going from where I was, straight as a door down to that table. To go down that ladder the men would have a spur on their shoes. Okay. Jake was with me. I went down there; Lord help me. Help me! I went down there, and I got my hook unhung and laid it free where I could pull it when I got back up on the track, then started back up that ladder. Jake was standing there looking over the edge, whining. He was worried about me. Mr. Dixon had missed me. He knew I'd been up there fishing, and when he heard Jake that man came running.

He saw Jake standing there, and he came running just as I was coming up to the top of the ladder. Oh Lord! Mr. Dixon said, "Where in the world you been?" Oh, he was hollering. He was a short, fat man. He was saying he just knew I had fell over and hung or something 'cause he'd seen the dog, and if I was in the water Jake would have jumped in after me. But Jake seen me coming up. He didn't worry while I was going down or either when I untangled the hook, but when I was coming up, he was just whining and panting. And something said, "Look back," then something said, "don't look back." Something said, "Look back," then, "Don't look back." Oh Lord. And I went up there, that ladder near about as high as a telephone pole. When I got up there, Mr. Dixon told me, he say, "I ain't never gonna carry you fishing by myself. I'll never do it no more." That lady, she said, "Let's go back home. I ain't staying down here with you. I'd rather lose every hook in town than to go down that steep ladder," she said. But see, I didn't have any other hook. I didn't.

But I can tell you there's some dangerous things you can go through and God will take care of you. He'll sure take care of you. Now there it was, all these items of danger God was looking out for me. He just wrapped his arms around me and said, "Let me take care of this fool. Let me carry her on back, 'cause I got something else I want her to do." That's all. "It's more here for you to do; I ain't ready for you now." Course you know, there was a time in the Bible when Jesus fled. Jesus run. Flee means run. And Jesus fled, saying "My time ain't yet come; I got some more here to do." So that's the way it was with me. I was going through the shadow of a death just like in the Twenty-third Psalm but my time hadn't yet come. And you go through it all the time but I went in it. I tell you, I went in it, and come out, too. Come out, baby. God is wonderful. Just tidied my life.

I remember in that camp there used to be a lot of singing and dancing but I didn't understand most of it. They were mostly Nassau people there, and naturally the music was Nassau singing and dancing. They did just like we used to do in my grandfather's time—beat tin pans and tin tubs, singing—"Beverley gal, I'll give you a licking." They say, "You're gonna get a licking," and that was a dance. We used to dance that thing. And we used to sing another little dirty song about "Mamma, mmmm mmm, guava jelly, young gal belly." I got that from them. Yes, Lord, I tell you, I loved myself some Nassau people—I call them salt-water people—and it seemed I just belonged among them, somehow. Some of my folks might have been there on the background, I don't know, but I love salt-water people. I was with them so long and so much until folks thought I was a Nassau. But then, I got along with them. I always got along with them. We got along good: never had to hurt any of them and I ain't never had them to hurt me. They were all good to me. I used to like eating crabs among Nassau, and other kinds of good things.

While I was cooking for that bunch of men in the camp a Nassau man told me one day, "Whatever you do, don't cook me no eel." I said to myself, "You been eating eel ever since I been here!" And he had been eating eel all that time 'cause I was cooking them. I'd skin them and save the hides—eel hides are good for cramps or anything else you want to use them for—then I'd slice them up good just like you do the catfish, and cook it right in there along with the catfish. And they didn't know it. I'd make them great big bowls of it, you know, eel and catfish mixed, and I hadn't told them nothing about it 'cause I figured it was alright. When he said that, I said to myself, "Well son, you been eating eel for the longest!" Those Nassau eat 'gator tails and turtles—they loved that but they didn't want no eel. Yet they were eating eels all the time—only they didn't know it.

There were some white men that worked down there on the Gulf. They were hairy and they ate the flaps off them stingrays. They'd take and beat them up just like you do conch, and I don't know how they cooked them but they ate them. They said they were good. Wasn't nothing but a flap—just like a conch. I used to wouldn't eat them conch, but I learned to eat them in Miami. They're good in conch salad but you got to know how to fix it. They real good.

But I don't like just all kinds of fish though. Now flounder, if I ever eat any, I just don't want to know it. If I don't know it, I don't want to know it because I don't like no flounder. I hates his looks. That's all. It's nothing in the world I know that lives in the water any uglier than a flounder fish. He too ugly. And I done heard such a bad story about him I don't want none. See, it says that God put a curse on him and that's why he's in that condition. But God just might have made that booger that way from the beginning; I don't know. But I learned that story on St. Simons, too. Say that flounder used to be the prettiest fish in the world. His eyes were so beautiful and his scales so pretty and he was so cute till he just put everybody else down, you know. He just twist around everybody, and looked over everybody; he was so pretty. He got to be too proud and God knocked his two eyes into one. Yeah, he knocked his two eyes into one so flounder became the queerest-looking fish. And they tell you that story so as to discourage you from acting cute. But they say flounder is a sweet fish, one of the sweetest fish in the water.

And I don't eat veal if I know it nor mutton if I know it. I just don't eat those things. I eat goat but I don't like that sheep or lamb. One thing I really can't stand is the scent of lamb. And the next thing, lamb meat is made like yours and mine. It's crossed that way, just like ours: a layer one way, then another layer the other way. A possum meat is that way. It's the same identical way. And the Bible say that a gopher—not the thing we call a gopher 'cause he got a long sharp mouth and he got a tail, that Bible gopher is a possum—the Bible say the pot should be broke that he's cooked in. That's right. No, I don't eat possum and I don't believe nobody should. My momma, she used to eat him. Many folks eat possum like he better not get around them. They say he's good. But the Bible say the pot should be broke that he's cooked in. That's all it is to it. And possum is the only thing I know on this earth that have intercourse in his head. And Momma and them would eat the head. You see, the he-possum is forked. He's made to go up her nose. And then, the little possum, when they begin to go to working, look like a little worm or a bait or something like that, then she sneezes them out into her pouch. That's right. That's the way they are. They're not supposed to be eaten. Besides, they eat more dead flesh than anything in the world.

Sam Sebourne was a good man, but after a while in Florida we went our own way and I met up with George Jones. He became my second husband and we traveled together from place to place for a few years following the crops. We traveled from Florida to Connecticut and all up there, most of the time on contract, and I always used to stop back here in Brunswick and St. Simons to see some of the people. Before we left, down in Florida one time

I heard a man saying that there was a bridge from Brunswick to St. Simons. I told the people right there that that man was lying. It was a bunch of men drinking and talking and having fun, and one of them was telling the others that he'd just come from Georgia—they must have come from Georgia, too—". . . yeah, man, and I hopped the bridge from Brunswick to St. Simons." I told them people that that man was lying, because couldn't no bridge go over there. But I wouldn't say it to the men, because they were dancing and singing and going on. So about two years later I was up in Miami and I heard some men talking about this same bridge. I came out there to the street where he was, and called him and asked him and he say, "Yes ma'am," and told me about the bridge they'd put across there. I couldn't believe it. George's father's brother was right here in Brunswick at the time and he hadn't seen George since he was five years old. So sure enough, when I came up here to see the people and George and me went to see his uncle we looked for the bridge: there it was. So we went across it. I was amazed. But see, I didn't know about these marshes and things that went straight across the South, and I couldn't see no way in the world for no bridge to go across that water.

We were on our way to Bridgeway, Connecticut, one time—we had a contract up there—when me and George stopped to see the Davis family. Cassius was dead and gone, but that family took in George, my second husband, just like he was Cassius. They're some good people on that line. Told him, say, "Come on and stay here. Stay here with us." I say, "George, we can't stay here. Ain't nothing here to make no living off." "Oh yes there is," he say. So we stayed right here. He said, "I'm going to build me a wheel here." So we stayed and now I'm glad about it. We went on up to Bridgeway but we came back and made this our home.

When we came to St. Simons there wasn't no farming here. I worked in these white folks' houses and hotels, tending children or being maid and cook. Sometimes I would be cook and take care of the whole home besides, 'cause when you got a job in those days you were often the maid, cook, nurse, and everything else. You had to wash and iron. Course most places they had washers, but you had to do all that ironing and that was lots of hard work. In those days blacks owned a lot of land on St. Simons. But in the passing years the children leave, and sell their legacy mostly. Black families used to own a lot of land around where the pier is now and the aiport. But the families have sold out or they're selling out—those who still own anything—to whites, and poor people who have their old houses there have to rebuild them or they have to move. It's sad in some cases. But anyway, when we decided to make our home on St. Simons we didn't give up traveling to work in different places. Momma came down and soon married her last husband, Mr. Julius and there was always a place for us here while George and me would travel with the harvests.

After my first child I didn't have any more until twenty-one years later, and he was born on St. Simons in 1935. My mother-in-law had sent word that I should get a good doctor because it had been so long since I'd had a child; and when it was time for the baby to come Dr. Chapman—he was on the Island in those days—he was there with me all night long. He stayed until the next morning and the baby still didn't come. He gave me four hypodermics, and after that there were no more pains. I was drowsy but I heard him call my husband and his momma in the hallway—I was at home—and I heard him say, "We got to kill one to save the other; that's the way it has to be done." Then I heard George—that was my second husband—tell someone we could always have another baby. So he and his momma had decided to give up the baby. They had to kill the baby; I heard that part. I understood that part, so I decided I'd stay awake to see what they would do. Then Dr. Chapman had to call another doctor—he couldn't do it by himself—and he called in the nurse that was with him. Anyway, in a little while Dr. Burke came over and they gave me a needle. I was drowsy but I heard Dr. Chapman say, "Don't give her much. I may have to work all night and I know how much to give her." He called the number. He was the one in charge.

I'd just bought four brand-new chairs—a rocker and three to set in—and Elizabeth was there, and all the other people were there with me, and they were fixing up to take the baby there in the house because I couldn't be moved. They didn't want any heart failure. So they were about to put me to sleep, and just before they did I told one of them, "I'm not in your hands; I'm in the hands of the Lord. If God intends for me to live, I'll live; if He intends for the baby to live, it'll live."

I hadn't had a child in so long I wasn't positive that I had a child. And then I didn't know if somebody had done some dirty deed, you know, so I couldn't have no more. I didn't know what it was. And yet I had asked God if there were any more children for me, to let me have them. I wanted children of my own. Anyway, they put me to sleep. And after a while Ms. Bea—she's dead now—she was calling me from the side of the bed, she said, "Wake up." I didn't know how long I'd been there because of the needle. "Wake up. Don't you know you got a big fine boy? Don't you hear him hollering?" He was in the other room. They had him in the other room and I could hear him hollering.

I said, "Who, me?" I didn't realize I'd had the child. She said, "They took it." And then I looked at the floor, and all the chairs were lying upside down. I didn't say anything, I just saw it, but she told me about it later. Chapman was a stout doctor. He was a stout man, and when he went to take the baby, to tear his head off—they take the head off first, you know, when they take a baby: break the neck and take the head off—God came between them and Chapman slipped. He fell backwards and that's why he knocked the chairs over. And then when he came back to take him, the baby came on. Ms. Bea said that after the baby came on, Dr. Chapman felt the neck and said, "This child's neck ain't broken." She said the doctor shook him and he made a noise and he kept shaking him upside down and the child was alright. Then Dr. Chapman went to shouting.

After he cut the navel string he went to shouting: shouted across the floor looking as though he'd had the baby instead of me. And that's why the chairs were turned over on the floor like that. Dr. Chapman said he was so glad, because out of twenty-three boys he'd taken, this was the only one saved. It's hard to save a boy when you're taking him, he said, much harder than it

123

is to save a girl. It's hard to save a boy. Anyway, God let my son live. He still has the scar from where they tried to take him, too, but he ain't ever had no trouble because of that. Dr. Chapman always came to see him—and the other children too—until the doctor died. He'd say, "Boy, you were born for some good work." Dr. Chapman was a West Indian too, but he and my stepfather were from different parts of the West Indies. He was the best doctor they ever had in that hospital that I've known. Anyway, George—that's the boy—he was named after his daddy, George Jones. He's a preacher now, and my pastor.

My baby son was born on G Street in Brunswick on the twenty-sixth day of December 1937, although I'd told myself I would wait until New Year's day to birth him after I didn't give birth on Christmas morning. Course I had walked all night Christmas Eve with a little girl who I had staying there with me—one of my first husband's cousin's child from the Island—and we had taken two or three turns downtown. I had a dime—it didn't cost but a dime to get a cab in those days—and I held that dime in my hand so if pain striked me I'd get a cab and go right on. That pain ain't struck all night. So Christmas morning came and they all had their big Christmases and I had mine too. I said, "Oh, well." Now in Brunswick, if you have a baby early New Year's morning, you get a prize. So I said, "I'm going to do that." I'm talking to myself: "I'm going to wait until New Year's morning and have the baby." But the twenty-sixth day was a Sunday and that's the day he came. Dr. Chapman came out to see me, and gave me some kind of medicine to hold me since he had to go and tend to another girl—a blind lady's daughter—who was in labor at the same time but she was closer. Then he came on back there with me. When the baby was born he came right away. The folks next door were still having Christmas right on; the doctor said, "What're you going to name him?" Now I had my mind fixed about that. I'd wanted a child named Cordell or one named K.C. I wanted that. So I wanted to name the baby K.C. in my mind. So I said to the doctor, "I'll have a name when you come back." He say, "Why don't you name him Joe, after his daddy's uncle?" And I said, "Okay," and went on. It wasn't until later, when I almost done signed his name at the courthouse—Joseph James—I thought, "Joseph! I don't want no Joseph in my house!" But it was written by then. And that's the way it be—you don't never know what you're going to do.

I was real young when my first baby was born, and I didn't have any more children for twenty-one years, but I was tending other people's children on and on, over and over. I used to go and get children out of the hospital and take care of them—friends I knew who didn't want to tend to their children, I would take them away from there, you know, 'cause if somebody didn't, ain't no telling what would happen. I've kept children two and three years, and then gave them back to their owner. Just to keep them. I just love children, that's all. And some of them have children and they want to go to dances, want to go this way or that way, they let the children stay with me. Just like my child. Some of them would do something for me, some of them never did do anything for me after I kept the children. I love the ways I find out among all children. Any color. I've never found any disrespectfulness about children, no matter what their race. Old people and little children, I just love to spend my time with them. I love it—right on! You can hardly find people older than me now, but yet and still I spend my time on them because I just love them.

And I notice a lot of people with their own children, and with my children too; you look into the manner of how children are coming up, especially in these days—it's a great difference in children coming up now than it was when I was little. It seems to me that there's always been little hardheaded children, always some kind of children who would be kind of disobedient and hardheaded, and when I was coming up they'd get a whipping and be punished for their hardheadedness. But I've noticed, since I've been along in this world, that all children don't need punishing. They do not. You have to watch children as they're coming up; sometimes they might be sisters and brothers right there in one house and everything, but some of them don't have to have the punishment that some of them have to have. It's important to understand their thoughts, their minds and brains, and the carrying-on of what they want to do whether they're bull-headed or not. Some of them will be ornery, some of them submissive, and like that. Some of them would like to show their parents, and some of them wouldn't care—they'd speak to their parents just like they would a dog and just don't care. And some of them will say to the other, "Why you say that? Why you talk that way to Momma? I'll hurt you." See, it lets you know right there that there's a difference in them.

They don't all have the same width of mind, the same width of brain, the same understanding; they weren't born under the same sign, and they're just different—that's all it is to it. There ain't no two that's just alike. I found out that some children, you don't have to tell them over two or three times about nothing. And some others, you have to tell them over and over again about the same thing. Some you have to all through the day give them a cutting or either a lecture or whipping or either a lick or something like that. And some of them all day long don't get n'ell. Don't have to have n'ell. But you have to watch that, you see. Don't put them all in one pan alike; just don't do it. I know sometimes the kids be out playing and one hurt the other one; he'll grab him and rub that place, you know, and say "Excuse me. I'm sorry. Don't tell Momma. Don't tell Momma." And some of them don't do that, you know. They won't do it at all. They want to settle up right away; they want to go run and tell their momma and sometimes they all get a whipping. But you watch them when they're out playing and you can tell what kind of children they are. I have them in droves sometimes, playing games, and I watch them and see how they act with one another. Sometimes I see there ain't no use in getting a particular one to join the games and I just let them stay over there. You can look across at them and watch how they look on you and how they act, and if you know children at all you could figure them out; you can just about judge how they ought to be and how they'll do. You got to know how to deal with people even after they get grown. Although there are certain folks that you can't deal with them. Nothing you can do with them, because once a thing is in the foundation, a person will just be that way. You'll come up that way, and be that way when you get grown.

I had one daughter—she's dead and gone now—and she got eight whippings in her whole life to my knowing. Unless the schoolteacher whipped her otherwise and I don't think so. I gave her eight whippings to my knowing. When she was a little bitty thing playing around the house, if something fell or anything happened, I used to talk to myself before I would whip her. She talked to herself, too, 'cause she grew up by herself. And a many a day, that way, she'd say no, I didn't do such-and-such a thing 'cause I told myself if I do that then you're gonna whip me. That was something. I remember the first whipping I gave her, that was a spanking. I got a little switch right across the back of her hand and a little whelp came there. She said, "Look what you've done." You don't know how far that hurt me. That went a long ways with me. She never knew it, but it went a long ways. I patted the whelp and rubbed it, and talked to her and told her she should listen when I say not to do something. And as for talking back, she never talked back at me in her life, in no way, shape, or form. And I had never talked back to my momma in no way, shape, or form. And I mean even when I was grown—of course I've never gotten that grown yet, even though I had children and grandchildren. My daughter was the same. She had children and grandchildren but she never talked back. She was just that same submissive way. And anything happened, then you know how to talk to them; you know how to speak to them.

But there are some who don't know from the beginning coming up: they're loose; they're slack. And I don't understand it sometimes. But you know, Jesus will fix that. Like when he had that woman with two nationalities in one womb—I forget her name but you'll find it in the Bible. She had two nationalities in one womb. God fixed it so they were twins, but they weren't alike—even in nationality. He can change anything. He knows how to make it and that's all there is to it. So I say this—whatsoever it is that you have, when you have children don't think because Jack can do such-and-such a thing so well that Tom can do the same thing all the time. They're different. Don't think

127

that if Jack's got such a vim for getting up in the morning and helping or doing something around the house that Tom is going to have that same vim. He may have something else.

And I look at them sometimes when they're eating—I love to feed children—and there's many of them who can let you know right away they don't like such-and-such a thing. They'll say, "Don't give me no okra" or "I don't want no onion." While another one, "Oooh, I want some onions." And sometimes when they get to teasing one another about what this or that one is eating I tell them, "Now listen: that's why God made so many different things. God made a heap of things so that everybody could have some of this and some of the other. And He's so good to us he put sweetening in it, and a flavor to it, so that midnight or foreday, you know what you're eating. You can tell by the way the food smells. And as sure as you're born, just as they don't like different things to eat, it's just as sure they ain't got all the same mind all the time."

And you see in some families where children would take the dog spirit and they would fight one another. They would hurt one another. And some others would stand up and say, "I'm not going to stay here anymore, 'cause if I stay, I'll hurt sister" or "I'll hurt brother. So I'm going to leave." So that's what I'm talking about; you got to watch yourself how you treat children. Don't expect all of them to be alike. Sometimes people would spend all the money they worked so hard for to send their children to school trying to make lawyers or doctors out of them. But if that doctor or that lawyer is not in his head, you can't put it in there. What's in there is going to come out. It says in the Bible that some men are made to be lawyers, others to be doctors, and some to be farmers. Some are made to build machinery, others again are pure indeed tailors. If it's in him, he can do it. And whatever he can do, then that's what he will do. Don't say, "I didn't send you to school to be no tailor." He'll be what he's going to be, and if you don't mind messing around there with him, he won't be nothing. He won't be anything because he'd be running out. You wouldn't let him do what he could do and there you are, he ends up doing nothing. And he could tell you what his desire is about certain things sometimes if you stay right there with him.

Like—I had a grandson. He's dead now; died right behind my daughter. He was so tall he was lacking three inches of being seven feet high. And they wanted him to play basketball. Oh, they wanted him to play basketball! They kept calling and calling. Some wanted him to play football or do the high-jump. And he could do it. He did some of all of it, but his mind was on something else. His mind was on them cars and machines. He wanted to be a mechanic. And when he got his mechanic work, he stayed there, and he worked and he was a good one, too. Yet he was tall enough to just pitch those balls in there if he had a mind to. He was like my Uncle Nehemiah, my grandfather's brother. Nehemiah was so tall until he didn't pay any tax. But it just wasn't in my grandson to be a ballplayer.

Now a lot of fuss has been made about children coming up in homes without fathers, and some people even claim that that makes them go wrong because they don't have any fathers in the house. I don't think that's necessarily true. If the father leaves the mother, or they're separated and he's not over them—or no other man—the mother has to be careful not to go astray herself. Sometimes she doesn't have to do nasty things to go astray. For instance, when she's trying to find work to take care of the children and not leaving them in good care, not being particular whether they go or come, and letting the children have their own way in every respect, and not taking care to see if the children bring something into the house where they got it from—the mother has to be careful against these things. If the child brings something into the house, you find out where he got it from or who gave it to him, and if he got it in the wrong place you make him carry it right back, and go with him to see that he carries it back. Now a child who ain't got a father might try to get away with such kinds of things, especially when at mealtimes with meals to be fixed the momma ain't there. Or, either, she didn't leave it in such a way the child could fix for himself. My husband died

129

when my boys were ten and twelve. Alright. I allowed my children to fix their own food, such as that they could fix. Like my great-grandson who stays with me now, he can fix his own eggs; he can fix mine. 'Cause you don't know what you may run into sometimes. If you have to go somewhere sometimes then they don't have to go hungry.

You almost make little girls out of them if they're little boys, but if they're boys and girls, you let them all be the same. You don't make the girl do all for the boy and then the boy runs out and do anything he want to do and come back. The first thing you know, he'll be gone astray. They got to be right there together, and if they ain't got no daddy, then you got to be momma and poppa with them and daily train them. You got to talk to them and teach them how they should treat theirselves. And just be as strict as you can be about how they treat people out there. And if somebody out there is saying something to the children that you don't like, you go to that person. Don't encourage the children in sassing them. Talk to the children, especially at nights when nobody's there. And if they have complaints about what certain people out there say or do, they should come home and tell you, because as children they don't know; they may have to go to that same door and knock for bread. They don't know what's likely to happen to them.

And another thing about it, if the children ain't got a daddy and the momma tries to give them everything they want—daddy could be there or not really—that leads to ruin. Because when the day comes that she can't do it, they're gonna get what they want somehow. She must let them know that they have to wait on some things; that they can't wear their best clothes all the time. Keep their mind right. Then you feel good about it. But if you're loose because he ain't got no daddy and you hate to tear his tail up, you might just as well say goodbye. And if you wait until too late, you might just as well say goodbye too, that's all it is to it. This is what I tell my granddaughter about their little girl; she's the only girl they have, and they're so glad to have her that they don't check her. But little girls are quick to ruin and ought to be checked in time. They're much faster to ruin than boys, especially if they find out they can have their way. And boys, when they get up around age seven or eight, they're just right for spoiling. You just got to keep a tight mind on them—not too tight—but let them know what you're doing it for.

There are some children on the Island, and my great-grandson used to go over to their house to play with them come evenings. The other day he wanted to go over there and I said to him don't go. "But Momma, they're my friends," he said. But see, I've never seen those children go anywhere to play. They have a very strict daddy. He's an awful mean man, and when he finds his children playing out of their yard or with other children, then they and their momma get in trouble. So I said to my great-grandson, "Don't go over there to play. If you meet them on the street or underneath the trees you can play with them, but don't go to their house." Alright. He didn't do it. But one day he went over there and came back looking drooped. I said, "What's ailing you?" He said, "Freddie them in the house and they can't come out." I said, "Didn't I tell you don't go over there?" Well, the mother had sent them outside, and the man came home and caught them out there and he didn't want it.

Course that's the wrong way to bring up children. We're up over children like a monster or a lion or elephant is over us in a way of speaking. When we grab one, he can't do anything about it. You're gonna whip him and he knows it but all he can do is holler. So in that way we're over them and we should realize that they want to play with children; they can't play with us. See, we ain't able to shoot marbles with them. It's alright for one to say, "My daddy shot marbles with me," but he's gonna soon want to play with other boys. And it's good for daddy to show them how to do things, but he should soon go on and let them have fun together. I know I just loved the day my grandfather used to play with us, and Poppa and Momma and all of them used to play with us; yet and still we children would get together when we wanted to just have fun. Because when they played with us we had to be real submissive; we had to play in a real submissive way. We couldn't just let ourselves go, because we were afraid we might do something wrong. That's just the way it is. And just like that man bringing up those kids now, and not letting them have a chance to be with other children, without a doubt some day he'll be sorry.

And I think it's the worst thing in the world for women and men to curse at their children, or curse with their children. Because when they get up to size and marry a woman or a man and that person curse them, they ain't gonna pay it no mind. They done heard that before. They come up with folks cursing at them and they don't care. Call them any old thing, it don't make no difference. You can't hurt their feelings. Like some women say, "I can't hurt that man's feelings; I can't make him understand me," or "I don't care what I do to her, she don't care." See, she came up that way. See with me, if I ever got angry enough with a person to set up and curse with them, we had to fight. That's all it is to it, because I figure then that's the time. And there are lots of folks the same way, too. Others just don't care a thing about it—"You ol' dog you!"—and they go right on about their business. They don't be studying about you; they've been called "dog" before. They know all about it and it doesn't worry them. White man call them that or anything, they don't care, because they've been used to it. But it's wrong, dead wrong, to curse your child, to call your child something out of their name, because you're him or her and you're cursing yourselves and your wives. You're cursing yourself altogether, because that's your child and he wouldn't be there if it wasn't for you. You're talking about yourself, then you're doubling up on yourself, because he wouldn't have been there to do whatever he'd done if it hadn't been for you. That's what I told a blind man one time.

He was sure enough blind, too, because the balls were out, but he was mean. I mean he was mean! He was a preacher, too— Blind Lewis Moffet was his name. He had married a woman down in Florida and that woman ran away from him. She had two children, but she ran away and left him and the children; she sure did, 'cause he was so mean to her. She went to Ohio. And you know, he went there and somehow or another found out where she was staying and got her back. He was a mean old rascal but there was something to him. If he came in a room and there was nothing in there but a crowd of women or girls and a man slipped in quiet-like, he would know. He'd sit there and cock his head like a dog and then he'd say, "It's a man here somewhere. Who is that man?" And you could tell him ain't no man there, but sure as you're born he'd know because he would smell it.

Anyway, one of their little boys was named Lewis just like him, and one day while he was still waiting to find out where the mother had ran away to, he got to beating the boy for something and told him, say, "You look like a fly on a bird dog." I said, "How do you know that?" He felt the boy and said, "I can just feel his face and tell that—just like a fly on a bird dog." I said "Did you feel yours?" And his daughter who was staying there said, "You ought to feel yours and see how yours feel. You must be the big bird dog." She was hot and I was too. And the little boy just standing up there looked just like him. I'll never forget that.

My second husband died in Tampa, Florida. He'd been sick for some time and I had to work to try to keep the bills paid and try to do something. So I wasn't there at the point when he was low. I was working on a farm contract up in Maryland, and had to go back and forth to see about him. He died on the 6th of May in 1945. But anyway, about a week before, I knew I had to go somewhere or something had to happen; I dreamt about it. I thought about George, whether he was getting better or worse, so I called down there to see how George was, and they told me he was resting good and feeling better. So I decided I would continue working and go home that next week to stay until something happened, and when I talked to the boss man he told me it would be alright, that I'd still have a job when I came back. Alright. I had a little chicken coop in the back of the yard where we were in Maryland with roosters and two or three laying hens, and right behind the yard was a little branch, and on the other side of that people used to catch groundhogs, or something that looked like funny little pigs. They used to eat them. I didn't. Anyhow, I used to think those things would be at my chickens.

I looked out there one night and through the window I saw a light going across. I had two rooms in the quarters. I slept in the kitchen and the children slept in the other room. I went into their room and the children were up. Joseph said, "Momma, I thought you were in bed." "Hush," I said. "Somebody out there trying to steal my chickens." I went in there and got my flashlight, and went outside to go around the quarters to get to the backyard. Whoever it was had to come through where I could see them, or go on through the woods. I flashed the light down there. I ain't seen a body. The dog was out there tied up and he used to bark a lot but he wasn't barking, so one mind said it must be somebody the dog knew. I went back in the house again, and a little later on before I layed down it came again from the same distance, the same direction. Just like a moon come on over. Sure enough, the next week I heard George was worse. It was his death. I thought somebody was stealing my chickens but I found out different.

# 7

# The Lord Fixed It

I WAS SINGING from the time I remember myself. I came up singing—in churches, and homes, and places just sitting around. We sat around together sometimes, just people, and enjoyed ourselves. Like at a candy-pulling or an egg-cracking party or anything; we would sing different songs. And in those days we would have setting-ups and singing when somebody died. It wasn't hard for me to learn the different songs, because we sang them over and over. And then some of them were part of certain games.

When I was in the world I did the blues and rags and things like that. I cake-walked and I waltzed but I did them with somebody who knew how. Somebody that really knew how because I wasn't that good. I was so fat and bowlegged until I'd fall out of there if I didn't stay up under those who knew how to guide and how to carry me.

I started out singing for money in St. Simons, but in Florida I used to sing at churches and I used to go to parties and sing. I wasn't a Christian then—I didn't become a Christian until I was near forty, and that was back in Georgia—I was in the world, and quite naturally we used to have our own little parties where we would swap songs and have fun. Somebody would sing a song and then another person would sing another song and we'd enjoy ourselves. I didn't like those parties with cussing, and flogging, and cutting up, and acting ugly. I didn't associate with that kind. I was down south, a little below Miami, with those Nassau. I was with them for about two years or more, and people used to think I was a Nassau 'cause I stayed right with them. But there was a lot of us there who weren't from Florida: we had Georgians and Carolinians and people from other countries and we'd do the same there as we did back home. We'd have parties for the church, and parties to help folks in hospital. We had dancing at those parties, too, though I never would. I preferred to play cards. I liked to play cards. Not for any money or gambling, but just for fun. Games like five-up and blackjack and coon-can (there were different kinds of coon-can) and other games of those days. And then we'd serve beer and whiskey and the losers would have to buy.

I used to love playing two best out of three with a partner. Whoever lost had to get up, then they would bring the whiskey. And we'd get a lot of whiskey because we put up a lot of partners. Folks used to be saying, "I don't see how in the world you'll drink so much." But we didn't. We'd have a little jar down under the table and we'd pour it in that jar. I wasn't drinking that stuff. And after a while the woman of the house would come by and we'd slip it to her and she'd carry it off under her apron and sell it over again. We had to look out for her. Remember—everything is a gamble. 'Cause if you sat there and drank all that, then you'd soon be out. No joke. It was fun playing those games. And at these parties we used to sing church songs, sing blues songs, sing anything.

And toasting was my business; I didn't want anybody to say a better toast than I said. I've seen folks hit their glasses and say nasty words, but that ain't no toast. That ain't none at all. I thought of toasting so that it looked funny to me to see someone get a drink and just take it up and drink it. That was just like not saying thanks at the table. When you go to take a drink, say something first. And so I didn't want anybody to get ahead of me with toasting, and if I could get it over I would. I'd get home and before I could sleep sometimes I'd be catching toasts. My mind would be at work. And I could've rhymed them, too, and write them down. I was writing up papers on them in those days. If somebody wanted a toast, whether it was at a party or a church or wherever, they would come to me and I'd write it up on paper, it didn't matter what the subject was. I quit that after a while, especially when I had to be in places where people weren't interested in that sort of thing. It makes a difference what kind of people you're with. See, a lot of times you'd be among folks at some big old bean farm where nobody ever talked about church; you just working, and ain't studying a thing. When you were living in a place where people were civilized and sociable and liked God's ways, sometimes they would come—children, grown folks, whoever—and ask me to write a paper. They could say on the word "air," it didn't make me no difference; I'd write it for them. Anything in this world that a person could name or say, I could make a paper for them and draw it out. I had that and I lost it. I left it. I just quit doing it and it got away. Just like you'd say making a poem, I call it writing a paper. I used to be able to do that on whatever subject you want, especially for the church. And I'd want it to rhyme.

When I came to St. Simons, John Davis and them were already singing here and I joined them. I started out singing with Julia Armstrong and them, but we never sang onstage. We were just in the hotel on Sea Island, or usually in people's homes. They sent for us to sing in different homes. Many of them like the singing and encourage it. There's a white lady here on St. Simons named Ms. Hanes—she used to be Ms. Icing—who got me to go to Atlanta, Georgia, to sing to her family. When I got there I met sixty-two head of people there, and that was the first time I'd faced such a big crowd. But on St. Simons the Coastal Singers was the name of the group then, and we used to have a pin with that name on it. Alan Lomax was the person who sent me out to the stage.

I first met Lomax in 1955 when he came to St. Simons to see John Davis and make a record. Lomax had been to The Cloister before and heard John sing, and then he'd met John in Waynesboro and heard him sing there. John loved to sing funny songs and those old-timey songs with rapping on the box and like that, and Lomax hadn't heard such singing in so long, couldn't find it anywhere he went like he found it with John, so he came to see John and get some more of that stuff. When Lomax came he met me in that group because John had asked me would I make a record with them.

We made that record but we weren't named the Georgia Sea Island Singers then. After that Lomax continued on talking with me and everything, and we went to Williamsburg to make that movie. The group was still singing here, and we were called the Spiritual Singers of Coastal Georgia because that's what Miss Parrish named it. She was the one who brought the group to white folks' attention, and she had a lot to say about where we'd sing, when we'd sing, how we'd dress and like that.

Anyway, when I began to get with Lomax and he had me up to New York to get the history of where I was from and other things for the book *Step It Down*, he turned to me and started talking about going places. I didn't want him talking to me about that but I didn't tell him that. In my mind, though, I kept thinking, "It doesn't pay for you to be talking about going places." Plus I had already prayed for it. He said, "Now what would you call yourself?" I had already thought to myself that I wasn't going to be no Coastal Georgia Singers because that was a lot of them people. I had enough sense to know I couldn't ride on their names. If I did I'd have to sing like they said sing and do what they said do. And so, well, I answered, "Georgia Sea Island Singers." Sea Island is coastal too, so I didn't get off the water. There wasn't anybody in the room besides Lomax, his secretary, and myself, and I named it Georgia Sea Island Singers. And it's been that way since, and it's going to be Georgia Sea Island Singers if it ain't nobody but me.

John and them went along with the name, took it like I said it, and when it came time to go out there it was "we" are the Georgia Sea Island Singers. They didn't kick against anything. And many of them are dead, but that doesn't mean the singers are all passed away because others have come in. There will be the Georgia Sea Island Singers as long as the children keep it up, even after I'm dead and gone. We have to have Georgia and the Sea Islands in the name because that's where it originally started from. Most of the singers in the old group came from St. Simons, but Mabel Hilary, she came from Atlanta. She married a guy from Sapelo and they came here to live. That's when she joined us. The George Cohens and Charlotte Reese sang with us here on the coast, but they never traveled anywhere. Other singers have and do sing with us from time to time but they usually have their own groups under their own names. Like Dan Smith—his group is the Dan Smith Spiritual Singers, but when our groups are on the same program he'll sing with us. We make a feature of singing together when we're on programs, because that makes a good program and we're all down-to-earth singers: flat singers is what I call it. We ain't singing no classical music.

When Lomax first got me started I traveled two years by myself—no guitar, no tambourine—and he didn't want the group, either. Then when I got out in California with Kate, who was my agent, I told them about the singers back home and what they could do. And the group back home had already said they'd be glad to come and sing if there was any way it could be worked out. So then Harold Darling said he'd send for four of them. I wrote back there and I called John Davis—whatever John said went—and told him about it, and John said alright and four of them came: Mabel and Henry and Emma and John. John was the one brought Mabel. She wasn't anything to him but she had a number of children and could use the help. She'd sung with us back on the Island when Lomax had us make a movie for CBS because she had a high-pitched voice which everybody liked and John had gotten her to help us sing. That was on the Island before I had left for California and I didn't quite know who she was; but John knew her, and when it came time to come to California he got her to come. The five of us put on some programs out there! Then I told Lomax about it and he asked, "What in the world did you do that for? Let those people go back home. Ain't nobody gonna be sending for a crowd of people that way." He went on terrible. I never showed John and them the letter. Anyway, we made some tapes and things and we sent him one or two tapes and he changed: "Before y'all go back home, let me know. I want y'all to come by here. Stop by here." Oh yeah.

And so we went to his place and we stayed there a week. He had the Mexicans and all kinds of people there to hear us sing. And ever since then he's been wild over us. But left up to him, I would've been right there by myself, self-concerned, and I couldn't stand it, knowing that they could sing and what they could do. And I needed help. He told me, "All you gotta do is get you another woman with you and get you a guitar. If you can't get the woman, get the guitar." He did all he could for me to learn how to play the guitar—paid a man three dollars an hour to teach me and I wouldn't do a thing but sit there and laugh at the teacher. So anyhow, after we stopped by his place, Lomax was crazy about that group. And that was the same group that had sang in Williamsburg, Virginia, and everything. But he couldn't see the group traveling as one. He was sure folks weren't going to send for them. And I wouldn't show them that letter, because I know how it would have hurted them, and they don't know up to today that Lomax spoke so deeply against them traveling and singing with me. But once he'd seen them, it was "My God! My God! They're thunderbolts!" He loved them more. And they traveled everywhere, Canada and everywhere.

After Lomax got me started going around, then people started sending for me. The first long-distance trip I made was to Berkeley, California; after that it was from one place to the other. People would come up and talk to me at these programs, and then the next week without my thinking about it, I'd get letters from some of them. It just spreaded and spreaded from one to the other. And in the beginning, I didn't think it would come to anything big, but God knows all. Anyhow I didn't push anything here on the coast at all, and some of the other singers got to talking. I didn't know what they might say to Mr. Alfred Jones about me singing over at Altama plantation: that's his place where he entertains his guests and business friends and others, and he called us regularly to sing the old-time songs there and show how they used to do in old plantation days. I didn't know what they might say to him about me singing with them, so every time they went to sing there, I would go. If they didn't want me to sing there because I was traveling I didn't have to, but I wanted them to know that I was right where I started at and it didn't matter. We weren't getting anything much anyway. Nothing but a little anyway. I may go out yonder and make a hundred dollars, come back here and I may make five. But it didn't make me any difference because I know that money isn't all. I was looking, though, for some of the darkies to raise the question about me going off to places. John Davis and them and Travis, they were going too.

Finally John, he quit singing down at Altama, because one night he was down there and got too high and the next time he went, Jones made him mad. Jones had the liquor there and John wanted it before the program. That was wrong. The liquor was there for them after they got through. Anyway, John got mad and didn't go back any more. Alright. Well, it got to where Mr. Jones called me. He was planning another big sing and he said, "I want you to kinda talk to the singers." That got me. "Last time they sang out there, they didn't act like they knew what they were doing." He knew how long they'd been singing—way back since before I came here—and that hit me, because I knew they didn't want anyone to tell them much of anything. So I was wondering, why ask me? Anyway, I just thanked God and so I said to him, "Have you told them?" He said, "No. But I want you to show them how to do it, and how they ought to act." And what he was looking at was Emma Ramsey and me, we would act like we were singers. We were singers. When we were there together, I'd touch her and say, "Emma, don't you leave me. You stick close to me . . ." because we could hardly stand it the way the others sang sometimes, going all off as though they're by theirselves and without care for the music or anything else. But we could catch one another and kinda sing it out. We were the ones who were pulling it up, and those white folks were watching that and I didn't know it. So, alright. I said, "I'll talk to them the best I can. . . ."

And now I had something on me. Sure enough. I didn't know what to do, because those people could've cussed me out. I would've had to tell them that Alfred told me to do it if they pushed, but they didn't push. He'd told Mr. Jerry that he'd asked me to talk to the singers, and Jerry had talked to the group and told them that the rest of them weren't pulling up like Emma and Charlotte and me and would they mind if I talked to them. I didn't know that Jerry had talked to the others. He's dead now, but when I came to talk to the group he said to them, "You don't go anywhere the right way if you don't have a leader. You take a mule and go out there and you may be going to Brunswick and that mule doesn't know how to cross the bridge, he's liable to carry you in the ocean or anywhere, 'cause he don't know how to lead."

The next week when we had the singing we all met early at Altama—we usually did that anyhow—before the white folks got through eating their oysters and having their meetings. Alfred Jones is into all these big businesses, you know, highway construction and the lights. He's one of those big men and that's the kind of people who come to see him. They have their meetings down there, their talks, and they crack oysters and have their dinners. So anyway, we were sitting up there that night and there I was. But I told them about it. I said, "Mr. Jones was telling me about us acting as though we're getting off, like we don't know what we're doing. And he says for us to act a little bit better." Then Ruth—George's wife—she spoke, "I don't know what he means saying we sing funny." I said, "I know what he means." I said, "When we go down, when it's time for us to march down"—all of them were there, the young ones too—"some of us wait until that time to put on our aprons, you see. And then we get out there and we just get together like ducks when we're supposed to march down two by two." It would be dark night out there but they'd have lights. And then I explained that if we marched down two by two or by threes, then our voices would blend better than if we marched with some folks a distance back, and I had to put it that way to show them what he meant. Our voices should be together. And another thing I told them was that I had asked about paying us a little more. I had, and he did say he would do that. But he had also said, and I hated it—I still hate it—"I'm going to pay you more altogether but don't tell the others anything. Their money will come just like it's been coming." I still hate it but anyway it happened.

His son would stand there at the door giving out the money after we got through; he had the whiskey and the money there. Those who wanted whiskey got it and everybody got their money. There were several of us who didn't drink. And when it was my turn to come through, "Yeah, Bessie, we had a good time tonight," and then he'd hand me my money in the same kind of envelope but my money was more. And they never knew the difference because I never told any of them; it hurt me, though, because I couldn't tell them. I got more but they were doing the same singing. But I couldn't reach out, because if I did then they would spoil themselves. And spoil me too. One member of the group—George Cohen—did say, "Mr. Jones must be giving you more money because he's telling you what to tell us." I said, "Mr. Jones is telling us that because we're not acting right. He knows we can act better." I didn't say he was and I didn't say he wasn't paying me more. What I told them was, if you're going to sing for fifty cents, do the best you can. If you ain't gonna do it, stay home. But what Mr. George said hit me all over, only he didn't know it. I just said, "Mr. Jones said that because we're not acting the way he wants us to act. When his people come, they come to hear some singing, to see some action of how it's supposed to be natural. They don't come to see us slagging back and acting like we don't know what we're doing." I didn't mention about that money any further, because Mr. George was sure on the nail. He sure was, but he didn't say any more about it. He got off the train, but he was dead on it. He sure was. And then I didn't like the way folks used to drink that liquor. After they got their money, they got a glass, then another glass of that old colored moonshine. But after I talked with them, we did it just like it's supposed to be done. Just like it ought to be done. And things went on.

Now when we got to Altama they tell us to do it any way we want to. And so that's what we do. The last time I had some children, and the people really enjoyed seeing the children play those games. See, I knew how far to go. We sang "Amazing Grace" and cut if off right at the solemn sound 'cause I didn't carry my tambourine nor clackers or anything. We do that sometimes, and when we do we talk to them beforehand to let them know. You see, some of the Baptist people don't like tambourines and some of the Methodists don't like anything at all—I'm talking about the Negroes—and I didn't want them frowning. The white folks, they ain't gonna frown at all. They enjoy it, and get right down with it. I told the children to keep their hands going and get their joy from clapping. They did it, and those white folks were clapping right along with them. So they had a good time. You just have to put yourself in it, that's all.

With the old group we used to get together and it was "You know this song here?" "You know this song?" And in just a few minutes we got that song going. We'd sit right there singing the old-time songs. We taught one another. I would've been just so happy if they could've layed off that liquor! I mean, until we got through the singing when we had programs. Then they could drink, get drunk and kick up their heels. But I just didn't like it on the stage. I told them that one day when they came in there with two or three great big bottles. Peter didn't drink the same brand as the others, so when they bought they had to buy separate bottles. And I asked Lomax, "Why you give them whiskey before they sing?" And he said, "Well, I'll tell you—your spirit's in you and their spirit's in the bottle." And that was true. They had to get the bottle. If they didn't see the bottle they weren't "gonna sing a so-and-so thing." It was no joke. They'd sit right there looking mad and sick. But you get them a shot in them, they were gone. So that's the way they did. Yes sir.

That drink, though, naturally led to another kind of problem—one that almost liked to kill me with that crew. You show them a contract, and show them what they do and everything, and then they get to drinking and talking with one another and they get to saying, "I didn't see it that way. Bring that contract here and let me see it again." They gave me fits. They'd say, "It wasn't that way; bring it here! Don't tell me, I know!" I'm telling you. And that's the reason why when we were getting money, I acted just like I do with Doug now. I let them go right on over and get it, 'cause I know what it is. Let them get theirs out and then let me get mine. And if anybody runs less, then let it be me. But Doug doesn't stand for that. He says if anybody runs less it will be him. John Davis was that way too: if there was two or three dollars left over, then John would just give it on to me. Both John and Doug would do that. But yet and still, I don't count on it. I ain't going to be giving out any money: "Here's yours and here's yours." It's the same thing that's on the contract but I want them to see it. That's all.

My main concern with the music is that it should go right, and that we should do right with it. Because if I should go and get a good hold, I want everybody with me to have everything equal. Some say you shouldn't do that. They say leaders should do so-and-so. And I tell them that this is not a church thing, you know. We just go on and we help one another. And if one stayed off for sickness—like if we were traveling and one got sick—well he got the same amount of money because he couldn't help himself from getting sick, see. Sometimes Mabel wanted to kick against that, but I'd say, "Uh, uh." If she were sick she'd get the same thing. Some will miss a day or two; don't worry about that. Those other folks ain't gonna worry about it. They gonna give you the same amount of money, and they ain't gonna take none from you.

The Georgia Sea Island Singers made three records—*Deep South*, *Georgia Sea Islands* Vol. I, and *Georgia Sea Islands* Vol. II. And somebody made a record of the Alabama Choir and put me on there. I've never sung with them in my life but I'm on their record. Then there's the *Step It Down* book that Lomax started but was finished by his sister, Bess Hawes. And there's a Rounder record with just Doug Quimby and myself and some children.

You had to know how to live with that older crew, but I miss them. John Davis is dead. Willis Proctor is dead. Mr. Ben Foster's been dead for a long time. Emma Ramsey was the last one to die. She died from a stroke. Peter Davis and Jerome Davis are still living but they don't sing with the group any more. Jerome, he went a time or two with us to Washington but he never went way off. They would come out and sing with the group, I guess, if I asked them. But they drink so hard I just ain't asked them. I was glad to get somebody with me where I wouldn't have to smell liquor on the stage all the time. They were really good singers but they couldn't sing without whiskey. They had that stuff going all out in the morning. And Mabel, she wanted to sing blues. Course we got rid of her on account of that and the drinking. Mabel was a blues singer and that's why they wanted to come in with the St. Simons festival 1977 as the Georgia Sea Island Blues Singers. Couldn't do it. I told them they couldn't do that. However else they wanted to name the singing after Mabel would've been good, but I said, "You can't name it the Georgia Sea Island Blues Singers because I named it the Georgia Sea Islanders and I never had blues singing in it." I told them that was the reason Mabel had to leave us, on account of her wanting to keep up blues and we didn't. We couldn't hang two in one that way.

Henry Morrison is dead too and he was the best one we had. He's the one who used to sing "I ask Aunt Dinah/Do her dog run rabbit." Charlotte Reese never traveled with us; Alberta Ramsey, she's been gone a long time. She's in Florida. On the record [*Georgia Sea Island Songs*] Nat Rahmings plays the drums but he wasn't one of our group. He was from Nassau. We picked him up in Miami and he just settled and made that record. On that same record Herbert Smith, a white man, is playing the banjo and Ed Young from Mississippi is playing fife. He's one who would sing with us when we're on the same program. Herb Smith too.

But now that time has passed on up, we have my grandchildren and other friend's children in the group, and Doug Quimby, who's completely into it. Doug is husband to the mother of some of my grandchildren—Frankie. She and my son Joseph used to be married but they're divorced now, and Doug is her husband. He'd been singing a long time with other groups, singing mostly gospel, but he knew some of the old songs and games and I asked him one day to go with me when I had to go traveling. I wasn't feeling too well and I asked Frankie did she reckon I could get Doug to go. She said that he had often wished he could go singing with us, so I asked him. And he's been there ever since.

He likes it and he's good at it. He's really good and that's why he's in there.

When we had the 1977 festival Mr. Alfred Jones, who owns Sea Island Hotel, just got completely stuck on Doug. He came up to me and said, "Now Bessie, when you come out to sing, I want you to bring that man with you." I said to myself, "You've already seen and heard this man," because I'd already carried Doug out there to Altama twice. You see, Mr. Jerry and George Cohen and them who've been going to Altama a long time, they usually step in front when we sing out there. Doug doesn't ever try to take over, and me, I'd rather lay right down beside them and go along. I know when it's wrong but I don't go over them, because I don't want them to be angry with me and get to saying that I'm trying to do this or that.

Here on the Island I'm a visitor. I'm a stranger. And it wouldn't make any difference whether I had been here twenty or forty years; I'm still a stranger. I'm talking about among the Negro people. They treat you well but you understand certain steps in there and you don't go too far. You go all around the pile but don't step in it, because the older heads that have been here a long time, they ain't going to have it. And so I just know how to get along with them and we're friends. I know I'm a stranger. Let me die and you'll see where I go. I ain't going to King's cemetery, no sir. I'm going to Strangers' cemetery, or out there at Rose Hill, wherever my children put me—but not in the others. We have a lot in Strangers' cemetery. And a number of people who we thought weren't strangers, when they died they went down there. They sure did. Cousin Clara's father when he died went there and I didn't know they were strangers. They came from Riceboro years and years ago when the mill was here. But they *came* here. St. Simons is a spot. You stay here long enough, you'll find what you are. The very young—those under thirty-five or thirty—I don't believe they feel that way about outsiders because they can't understand any of this.

Course the white folks out there, if it suits them then it suits me because we're all singing for them, and I don't try to make anyone look little and don't want them to make me look little. So that's why Alfred Jones didn't recognize that Doug had been to his place. We just went along with what they were doing, that's all. But over at the festival when we were singing together, you had to know Doug was there.

I'm trying to get my grandchildren to carry it on out—the songs and the games and the way of singing—but if they don't then I'm going to get somebody else. I told Doug the other week when we were in California, I said, "Every time that clock ticks, I'm getting older." I said, "Now I want to get someone to help you, because you're the only one here who's grabbed ahold of the thing and know what to do." I said, "You get someone to help you and maybe they can hear you and they can go on and help us." But I want to settle this now. My granddaughter Vanessa is good, and when we go onstage or go to a singing, she goes with us but she doesn't take over anything. That's what I want her to do, take over something in the songs or play-leading. But instead of being that way, she stands there hitting on the tambourine. Now I just can't keep standing there talking to her after I know she knows what I'm trying to do and say I want to see her do it. I want to see her talent. Hitting the tambourine every once in a while and helping sing, that's not it. You got to know how to do it. That's what I'm asking, to get someone to just go on through with it and help Doug carry it on out, 'cause he can't just do it by himself.

Frankie does all she can. She's good on that book work, that pencil work. She can cover that money and she knows how to deal with different kinds of people. She's one of those cunning women, and the Bible says you got to be cunning to get where you're going. So that's what I want them to do whosoever gonna do it. Okay, now if I should get someone else from outside the family, they'll say why should I get someone else? I told them this some time ago, I said, "I got enough offspring to make a Jones band of singers." Course some of them could learn how to play the harp, some could learn how to play the guitar, others could learn how to play other things. And anything they might want to know, then I'm willing to help them learn it, you see. And there are places in Brunswick where you can go to learn to play anything. These people teach it. And I told them they should go on and do it, but they ain't got time for that.

I could maybe get someone from the children and grandchildren of the old crew, like John Davis's people, but I haven't tried that yet. What keeps me back is the drinking. The biggest thing you could get in Frederica is that same old sixty-six—that drinking. I don't know any of them up there who don't care for that drinking. Anna Pearl and Emma, they're both good but they want that liquor. Now with both of them, if I talk to them about not drinking before we go onstage to sing, they won't do it. But the thing about it is I don't want to have to do that. Yet if they go with me singing, I sure will. I'd talk to them privately and say, "Now y'all don't drink, cause when the people smell the liquor, they won't want to pay us." I'll just say it in that way. Not that I don't want to smell it, or that I'm ashamed of it, 'cause whiskey is made to drink. But there's a time to drink it, and those that want to drink should drink in the right way. And see, I don't want any argument, 'cause sometimes they'd say words quicker and faster than they would if they weren't drinking. And yet and still, they won't mean any harm. They'll be telling one another, "Oh, so-and-so," just a bad word right quick. A slack tongue. And all that doesn't work with me at all. But yet and all, there are some good singers up there. They are some singing people in Frederica!

There's a boy up there and I wanted to get him. He's in church, a Christian boy, and when he was about twelve years old, I mentioned about going to get him and heard some of them say, "Oh, don't think you're gonna carry my child away off from here. Noooo. Uh, uh. He ain't been going and he ain't going now." And so I didn't try any more. But that boy can go. Right now he's sixteen and he's still in church but I didn't bother with it any more. Because if they won't let him do it, then just let it alone.

Morrison had one son, and I don't know much about him exactly but I heard of him. The Ramseys, Emma and her sister, both have children, but all of them are high drinkers. All I know of. It's hard to get somebody who can stand up and do it, but they can sing. They sure can. But then there's another thing, I can't depend on them. You know you can't depend on no young drunks, 'cause if they want to go today they'll go for a certain amount of money, and then the next time it's "How much in it?" Yet you'll hear many of them saying, "I'm black and I'm proud." Most of us certainly are proud but don't understand it that we ought to be proud. 'Cause one thing about it, you should be proud about it if you're black because it's honest. They tell you that black is honest, and so you should be proud of it if you're black and no changes to it. A lot of them just say so 'cause "I'm proud" means I ain't worried about you; I'm up-to-date. I got my money—or either a little change since they never get a whole lot—and I can go without you. But see, black can do it, 'cause it don't take much to take care of a black as it does for a white. Black can go along and feel happy off ten dollars in his pocket, whereas a white man would be worried to death 'cause he ain't got nothing but ten. He'll worry about what he's going to do tomorrow and don't care how poor he is, he's going to try to look for some more money, 'cause see, he wants more money. That's all it is to it. He'll stick you up and take it or he sure will kill you, because he ain't proud without the money. But see, we're proud with a dime. What I mean by proud is we're happy.

You can make yourself happy; you can make yourself miserable, money or no money, because money does not enrich us. You may be rich with money but money is not riches. Riches is when you got something within you that you own right there. I'm proud because I know I belong to God. I'm proud because I depend on The Man that owns everything. Sometimes I tell people that I can stand up in my riches and turn around in it, 'cause every way I turn it's God's work; it's God's world. I don't care what I do, it's God's work. And when the way looks like it gets rugged with me, I have this to think about: Jesus had this before. Jesus went through this before. And God carried him through it. Why not me? See, I got to go through it too. You meet some people say, "I ain't gonna take it; I ain't gonna do it; somebody got to die 'cause I'm gonna get me some money tonight. When they go to bed I'm gonna tear down the back; I'm gonna go in their house; I'm gonna burn their house down." Well you're in bad shape when you come to that. You done throwed your pride just down. You done flatted yourself. 'Cause when they catch you, brother, it's too late. It's just too late to holler about it and cry about it then, 'cause you done done wrong. That's all.

I was at a camp once when Pete Seeger came and asked me to sing at Carnegie Hall. That was the first big stage I'd ever been on in my life but it came naturally. I could see that Pete himself thought I was shy, or scared. And I heard one man say, "Ooh, I ain't going out there. Ooh, I'm nervous. I've been singing for five years and I still go out on that stage nervous." And I looked at him and thought, why should he be nervous? He was a white man who played a guitar by himself. I thought to myself, "He's got a guitar. If I could play a guitar it ain't nothing I'd be nervous about." I don't ever remember being nervous, and if I were I just wouldn't go. That's all there is to it. I wouldn't see the need in it. If you're afraid, then you better go and hide. That's the way I see it.

But whatsoever it is, do what you can. You may not do what you want to do but do what you can. And I've always had it this way with myself. I asked God for what I'm doing. I asked God long before Lomax called me, I asked the Lord for me to come out. I didn't know how I was coming out, when or where, or who I was coming out with, but I wanted to come out and do something because none of the people had left anything here. And I wanted to leave—when the Lord takes me out of this body—I want to leave something here of me. Fact is, I told the Lord, and I meant it, I never want to die. I never, never want to die. When the world folds in, I want to be here, in my work, in my doings, and with the people, among the people. They don't see me but they can see of me. Now that's what I want to do. See, I just wish sometimes that I could see that handwriting or something from my grandfather and people of his time, some-thing that they had done. So when I have anything that belonged to them back there now, I feel good about it. And I like to show them that I'm holding up their songs, holding up their doings that they told me about. That's great to me. They didn't write it down but I know they did it. And I didn't know whether it would get written down!

After I went to Carnegie Hall, I just continued on. People in the schools would call me, and that was fun. So I asked God to let me do it, and He sent somebody for me and the place where he knew it could be done. All I said was, "Lord I want to come out: I want to do something. I just don't want to die, I truly don't." And He knew how to do it.

# 8

# Spiritual We Are

I BELIEVE WHEN it comes time to give that body back to the dirt, preparations must be made so that inward man would be clear. And when you get worried, troubled and scared like something's gonna bite you, or somebody's gonna shoot you in a minute—when you get so scared you can hardly go to the next room—that's that soul crying. That soul inside needs attention. And now the devil says, "You go get you a big drink and that will stop that," and then he just run it up so that worry can come again. But you've got to see the other man. Let him come in: let the spirit of God come in and that will clear it up completely. But you've got to hear what God says. I myself was tested with Him twice. Once when I was in the state of Maryland on the eastern shore, and which before I left home I was intending to help build a church for our group—the Church of God—that had started having meetings in my house.

In those days I'd been traveling with George, my second husband, who was an agricultural man before he took in sick and died. I had to work for the children, and the best work I saw then was right in the agriculture business so I stayed in it, and I was at a canning factory in Maryland and staying in their quarters. Those quarters were no place for me, particularly with my two boys. Nobody told me anything, but I knew those quarters weren't for me. I was working there but I wasn't quite like the rest of them. I just didn't agree, that's all. It was just a wrong place. But I worked, trying to get some money so when I came home I'd have something. And so I was nipping and grading beans, taking the ends off beans and sorting them at this time—though I had done every kind of work in there down to driving the line and everything—and we used to sing church songs. Different people from different places—I was the only one from St. Simons—but we'd sing those good church songs. We'd start a song and crowds of people would join in. It sounded so good, you know, we just sang and sang while we were working—pretty sound—and white folks just listening to their factory ringing with nigger music and the machines running and it's going. But something said to me, "You ought to have a church just like this: you should have them singing in church just like this. You got to do it. God wants you to do it." So one day there were about eighteen of us on the line and I got a letter from Elder Hunter saying he'd be glad when I came home so we can try to build a church. That was on my mind, alright, but I was still pressing against it.

Then another day I was working on the line, making tomato puree, tomato paste, and tomato foods and stuff, and I could see some of the other workers talking to one another saying, "Not me child!" There were about twenty-five of us in that little bunch, and I could hear them hollering, "Not me!" and I wondered what was the matter. My two boys were on the top running cans. According to the government they weren't supposed to work, but when they came in from school the man would hire my boys and another lady called Butterfly—she had a birthmark like a butterfly—her boys and mine were the only children working at that time. She was a quiet, good woman, tended to her business, and she made her boys mind. But those four boys were up there and I thought maybe something happened to the children. People were still talking, "Child not me; shut my mouth," "Hush, don't say nothing," and I was still running the line watching what happened, until finally here comes the boss man with two white men. Those men had been trying to get to me all that time but nobody knew me. Everybody knew me but nobody knew me.

They thought since I came from the South and they didn't know what had happened, they figured it might be something that would put me in jail so they wouldn't say that they knew me.

So anyway, here they come, the boss and these two white men, and he says, "These two men want to talk to you." I said, "Okay, I'm coming. I'll talk with them." And that was my money—eleven hundred dollars from the insurance people. The Lord told me, in a way of speaking, there's your money, go home; build your church. So I got my two boys ready—Joe the baby boy and George the older—and got them both tickets to travel on the bus so I could travel on the truck with the other workers and bring a lot of that stuff I had. I had peaches, apples, cucumbers, and all kinds of stuff—almost a half truckload myself. But Joe wouldn't ride with George on the bus by himself: "I ain't gonna ride; you got to go with us." George said, "Momma, I'll go," And so George left on the bus that would get him home to St. Simons long before we would, and I got on that truck with Joe and the other men and women and all that crowd. It was a crowd of us on there! But we wagged it on in here, and they brought me all the way to St. Simons' cause they wanted to see the Island.

There were nine of us when we got there, and Momma fixed dinner and we had a nice time. Well I had to go to the outdoor toilet—that's all we had then—and while I was out there something said, "You ain't got enough money. Give that money you got to your momma, all but seventy-five dollars, and you go on down with them, 'cause where they're going there's lots of money and you can make enough to help build the church." Something said, "Don't do it." I came to the door of that outhouse and I stood there and looked. I couldn't get my mind right to ask God what to do. Something said "Do it" and something said "Don't." Finally, it whipped me out and I decided I'd go on and try two weeks anyhow down there and see if I could make some more money. Money's not all, baby! So I gave Momma all my money except seventy-five dollars, just like He said, and I boarded that truck. I went down there and let me tell you, I'd never been in such a bad place in all my life! It was a bad word for good morning!

The place up in Maryland was bad enough but it was nothing compared to that one in Florida. That was truly a testing place there. The water in the pump was pulled over a graveyard and everybody was getting sick off that water. Bad weather, and foul cussing. All in the fields it was "kiss my so-and-so," "your mother." All day long Mr. So-and-so cussing with Miss So-and-so, even cussing at beans! It was sad. Not much fighting, but just an ignorant, dirty crew. I thought, "The devil has put me in it now; Lord have mercy!" I got acquainted with one good woman there named Frances. She and I did have some fun, and when I managed to save some money, I gave it to her to keep 'cause I was afraid to keep any money in the little room I was in, because those women were rough and you didn't know when they'd break in and search your place. That was a nasty crew around there: some women slept with women, and some men with men. I'd never seen such things. I wanted badly to get out of there. Anyway, after about two weeks and two days I went fishing with Frances and I fell in the water.

Sometimes I think about it and it just gives me the creeps. I had set my pole on a rock to bait my hook again—the fish had eaten off the bait—and I baited it and threw the line back out there. I was sticking the pole up underneath that rock when the rock went over. And I went over. Frances, who was there with me, she heard the splash, and when she came she had a pole drawn back to throw to me—she knew I had fallen in there—but I was already coming up on the side of the bank. When I got up on the side of the bank I was laughing. She said, "Woman! You fall in this canal and you come out here laughing?" I told her, "Just as well laugh as to cry." She said, "Let's go home," and we went on to the house. She didn't know my mind. You can walk along and talk with God and nobody hear you. And when I did, He said, "It will be worser next time if you don't go back and do what I told you."

The seven o'clock bus next morning couldn't get in too soon for me. I packed and wrestled all that night not to go to sleep so I could be on that bus. Nobody knew it. Next morning I called Frances and told her, "I'm going home. I'll write you when I get there." Later I wrote and told her all about it: how come I had to fall in that canal and God brought me out. You don't play with God. That canal was so deep, the drag-line couldn't hardly touch the bottom. I fell head over heels in there and had never swam a lick in my life, but I'm here and I ain't no spirit. God brought me out. He's got a way of whipping you and He's got a way of bringing you out. "I ain't gonna let you drown; I will do you like I did Jonah: put you down there, and you're coming out." You've got to hear what God says. I asked Him a favor and He did it; then Satan comes in and he tried to show me another point, another thing. But if you let Satan override that good spirit, then you get messed up. I did it. He said, "It's going to be worser than that if you don't go and build that church." That's what He told me and I didn't ask anybody's advice. I told God, "I'm gone," and I did like Jonah when he got out of that whale. I took a beeline to the Island. That was on the 11th of March; I got home on the 12th. Elder Hunter came to see me and we talked over that church business and on the 13th of March we started right on there.

We had a meeting at my house again, then we bought a tent. The tent took up enough from time to time to buy that lot that we've got. After we got the lot, we had to get the lumber and all the other stuff, but we had enough members to help out with that. Now, who was going to build the church? And behold, we couldn't get anybody to sign a contract to put up that building. We didn't have the money, and nowhere to turn for the security. The preacher's word didn't go, the deacon's word didn't go, nothing. Then they tried going to a lawyer, and he came to me one day and said, "Mrs. Jones, you can build that church down there. If you get you two more trustees, then you can build that church." I said, "Me?" I said, "I ain't got no money." He said, "I know it, but with your word you can build a church." That got me. "Just get you two more trustees and write it down and bring it to me over to the court and you can build that church. If you had a husband you couldn't do it." I was the mother of a church and I didn't even know it, and with a requisition I could build. See, he said that mother stands when that preacher's gone. You can turn the preacher off or he can get mad and leave, but with that mother, that church is gonna stand. I didn't know that. And that's how I came to build our church.

During the building once, I remember, we needed some more lumber. I had thirty-two dollars and that old dry wood cost thirty dollars and twelve cents. So we got the lumber and took it there that evening. Next morning we didn't have a piece; everything was gone. A little later on we could hear the hammering, and they built a little house. But God doesn't like ugly. That house burned down, they done died, and all little things like that just happened. We finished the church and it's still standing. You see, He doesn't like ugly. We got some more lumber and the lumber-yard didn't charge us any more when I told them that somebody had stolen what we had bought. It was no use fussing, because many folks were building then and you couldn't walk up and say, "This is my lumber," because you ain't got no mark on it. But I knew where some of it went. You see, when I was borned again—and this goes until the Lord takes me out of this world—I told the Lord not to let anybody in this world give me nothing. Nothing. No way. And anything that they took from me, don't let me try to get it back from them.

Everything is owed to God. But whatsoever people may do for me, Jesus, you pay them, because you know more of what they need than I do; you know how to pay them. No matter how rich a person is, God can pay them. He did it. He done done it so widely that right now a very rich white woman is telling me that she wouldn't have had so-and-so if she hadn't helped me. She's a millionaire; she's the one who bought me the home I'm in. She has orchards and vineyards and all that kind of stuff in California, but her blessing came because of me. He'd never have blessed her if she hadn't needed it, and I didn't even know it was happening.

When I went out to California to sing on Lomax's recommendation, an agent there by the name of Olivier sent for me. He said I should ride the airplane, but I didn't go that way. I prefer riding the bus, so I rode the bus five days to get there. While I was out there different people used to come to get me to sing, and that's how I came to meet Kate. Kate and her husband had took over the business from Harold Darling—he was one agent who used to get us big jobs, and the same one who finally sent for the other singers from St. Simons—they took over his business when it went down and they gave us a place to stay while we sang at the Ashgrove on Melrose Avenue in Los Angeles. We stayed there about a year before we came back home. Kate's husband was gutting her, 'cause she was rich. You know how folks come on talking about love and all that, but he was just using her. Well anyway, she was finding it out and she was getting rid of him, but I didn't have anything to do with that. That was their business and had nothing to do with me. But she was my manager and wanted our help out there, and they gave us this whole house and we were staying in it, cooking and eating as we wanted. Then when I came back to Georgia she wrote us and called from time to time, and finally said she wanted to come east.

Now I didn't know her mind or anything about their business. We'd been to Resurrection City in Washington, D.C., and I'd stayed three weeks with our manager there—a man named Ralph Rinzler. That was when they had all that flood, and water covering everything. I didn't know that Kate knew him, or that he knew her. But she came to St. Simons and was staying with one of our friends, because I was still down there in Harlem, in the slums, in a little room with my stepfather, Mr. Julius—he was a Dutch West Indian, the only one around here, and he'd been so good to Momma we couldn't leave him alone or put him in an old folks' home. We had been living in that house for twenty-seven years, but they were threatening to tear it down. So I told Mr. Julius one day, I said, "We got to move out; these folks're gonna tear these houses down." "No, no. They ain't gonna tear them down," he said. "Don't believe them. They ain't gonna tear them down." "I'm sure they're gonna tear them down. . . ." "No, no," and sure enough they never tore those houses down! But anyway, we didn't know then, and folks were moving and getting out.

I could've gotten a project room for eight dollars a month since

I had no husband, but I didn't want to move to Brunswick and live in the project. I wanted to stay on the Island. So Kate came. She came just before Christmas, in time for our Christmas program, and we had her in it. We had a good time and she liked working with us. She stayed all of January, going to the beach every day, and she got acquainted with some white people from the North and that made me feel good for her. Then my son gave her a big oyster roast and some of the other people, they gave her crab boil, and we had a good time. My son would also carry her around after his work to all the different places on St. Simons and Jekyll Island, so she had a good time. Now when it came time for her to leave, something told me to ask her to let me have enough money to pay down on a lot. My mind was this: if I got a lot paid down on, and got the deed squared, then I'd be able to get a house built and Mr. Julius and I could stay there. I knew I'd have to work like the devil to pay for it but I was gonna do my best—me and God—even if I had to go without some eating. All I wanted was a place to stay. Alright, I told myself to ask her. Something said, "Don't ask her; she ain't gonna do it." And something say, "She can't say anything but no." So we were walking out the evening before she left, and so I said, "Kate, I want you to let me have enough money to own a lot"—I was on my way to California behind her to work at the Ashgrove— "and when I come back out there next month I'll pay you back your money. I want to pay on a lot so I can get the people to build me a house, because I've got to have somewhere to stay."

She didn't say nary a word. I showed her an open lot and told her what the man wanted for it. I showed her some other lots. And then we came to a lot with a house that used to be a beauty parlor, but the girl had quit dressing hair and her mother had added two little rooms and turned it into a dwelling house. So we looked at this house—there were a man and a woman living there—and I said, "This place is to be sold but the woman wants cash for it." Kate looked over there at it—she hadn't said a word yes or no 'bout the other ones—then she said, "That's a good-looking house. You and Mr. Julius could stay in there and your grandchildren." She said, "I'll buy that for you."

I had said, "Loan me some money on that lot," but that was the heaviest "I'll buy that for you" I'd ever heard in my whole life. Nobody had ever said anything like that to me. I didn't know what to say. But then I had my way of asking God to speak for me—which I did—and said, "Kate, all I can tell you is, the Lord will pay you back. 'Cause I promised God not to let anybody give me anything and I meant that. But God will give you fourfold for what you did for me. God will give you the desire of your heart."

When I said that she dropped her head and said, "I hope He does." And I, not knowing her mind, but struck by her words, wondered what her trouble was.

When we got down to my son's house everybody was there, but something told me not to tell them anything. Because, then, if she didn't do it, nobody would know anything. She had said she was going to give me a check which I should take to the lady and tell her that the rest of the money would be paid the next month. This was the 9th of February and I was going to California in March. Alright. The woman who owned the property ran the undertaker's parlor in Brunswick, so I went over there and told her, I said, "Miss Hall, I want to buy that place and this is all the money I got right now. I can give you this check on it and next month I can pay you for the whole thing."

She looked at me—she was getting a body ready to be sent out—and she grabbed me, almost picked me up. She said, "Oh, I'm so glad it's you, honey! My momma will be glad in her grave." She said, "I was born in that place and I didn't want anybody selling whiskey, having parties, and carrying on in it; I know you ain't gonna have that. I'm real glad you got it." That was something to me. That struck me. Anyway, I went on to California. I hadn't told anybody anything.

About two weeks after I was out there, my son George called. "Momma, that woman that was here with you, she sent a check here for Miss Hall; say it's something about a home for you or something like that. Did you know about it?" I said, "Yeah." He said, "Miss Hall doesn't know whether that kind of money is there or not—it's three thousand dollars but she's gon see." I said, "Alright." Then I called Kate. I hadn't seen her yet, because she was on Sunset Strip and I was at the Ashgrove, so I called her. She was in a hurry and she said, "Oh yeah. Alright. I don't blame her, but she'll find the check's good. I'll see you." I said to myself, "Ain't this something?" Then I went talking to the Lord again. I had some of the group with me but I couldn't tell them anything so they didn't know. And I went on.

So my son met me when I came home; he had the deed in his hands. Children are a sight! That deed read, "George L. and Bessie S. Jones," George at the top. That's the way he set the deed—George and Bessie Jones. I guess he said since I didn't tell him anything he was gonna fix me. Course it's gonna be his one of these days, but I wouldn't have put it like that unless I had asked Momma. Anyway, I haven't changed it. I looked at it sometimes and started to change it but thought, no need. No need to change it. He's liable to die before I do. My daughter died before I did and that just shows you.

About a year after that I was in Fox Hollow, a big camp outside Albany, New York. We were there taking part in a big program. And I was sitting at a table eating when a man came up from behind and hit me on the shoulder, and when I looked back it was Ralph. He was eating and he had his food in his hands. I said, "Sit down and eat." He said, "No, I ain't got time. I'm going to California to see Kate." I looked at him and thought, "Our Kate?" Because while I stayed with Ralph in Washington the only women I saw around his place were hired to do something. I never heard him talk about a girlfriend. Then came July and I was up at Plummet, Massachusetts, singing for May Gadsen when I heard that Kate was coming to see me, and that she and Ralph were married.

So a Friday Kate came, and Ralph with her, and the devil told me, say, "He's gonna make Kate take that place from you." But anyway, Kate and I went for a walk in the meadow between some bushes and little wooden houses, and she said, "Bessie, you remember the day I told you I'd buy that house?" I said, "Yes, I do." She said, "You know you told me God would give me fourfold for what I gave you?" I said, "I sure do." "And you remember you told me I'd get the desire of my heart?" "I sure do." She sat still, didn't say anything, but water came streaming down her face. And I liked to went to crying though I didn't know what for. She said, "He did it. The Lord gave me Ralph," and she fell on my shoulders. "I'd been fishing at Ralph for eight years." And I thought of how to get her to laughing because I didn't want to cry, and I said, "Well, Kate, I wouldn't fish at a whale that long," and we got a laugh out of that.

She said, "You know what? My brother gave me an island in Massachusetts with thirty-five families on it." She said, "You know, that island is bigger than the little house I gave you and I didn't have any need for it. That's more than fourfold." And then . she got Ralph, and they're getting along well.

You see, she needed somebody to love her. That other husband was killing her but Ralph's rich; she's rich; they didn't marry one another for their money. Ralph needed somebody that needed love and he needed love. He hadn't married anybody because he couldn't find anybody to love him like he ought to be. And we're all in the glory because God did it. I asked Him, and I didn't know what He would do, but He did it.

I love to travel, I really do. I love to do what I'm doing because it seems to be reaching so many people. Some people, look like that's what it took to reach them. You don't know what kind of an answer sometimes a person might want. Just say, you don't know where it's going to fall at and how it's coming to you. And so that's why I say, "Thank God for it," 'cause what I'm doing and what I've done have reached a lot of people that I wasn't expecting. They write me letters and say, "Since you told me such-and-such a thing, since I've learned such-and-such a thing from you, I've overcome."

And lately, here not too long ago, a white lady whose son was a great dope addict, she came here. I had met them about three years ago in Pennsylvania but their home was in Chicago, Illinois. His wife was a black woman and both of them were dope addicts. Young people. They were on that mess and they were a mess! And she was as nasty as she wanted to be. You know, dancing and wiggling and woggling so she could get money out of other men for him and her to buy dope. And he knowed all that kind of stuff about her. It was terrible. Anyway, from singing with us—he was on the same program and just had a good time singing onstage, and me thinking nothing of this—something in it reached him. Now I do speak about these things when I'm in front of people: How you treat yourself, and how you should take care of yourself and make what you want to be out of yourself. So then I was speaking about the dead trees and the live trees, you know—the dead trees need to be cut out of the way of them live trees—and was just talking from one thing to another not knowing anything, and then I went on to explain about how the Lord had blessed me to stand up among all them good live people and everything. You know, you can act live and you're dead, just as dead as you can be. And so I talked about all those things.

After the program was over, he came in the little dressing room. I went to get some water, and after I came back we were talking and having fun about what different ones had said and done and so on. And he beckoned to me. I went to him. He said, "I want you to pray for me." He was shaking. He says, "I'm in a mess and I need help." One thing struck me, and that was the only thing, that one word—I need help. And I knew that was true. 'Cause you can get in a bog sometimes. You be driving along fine and good, but then that thing strikes a bog. When that happens don't blame the thing that's in there; try to help it out. Maybe it won't get in there again.

I wound myself up in that young man right there when he spoke that one word. And so some of the people there were pulling me, touching me in the back, touching me in the front, but I didn't pay them any mind. I acted like I didn't feel it and continued on talking with him. I was a little shy with him in a way, but something said, "Don't be." I had heard that they do so many funny things and he just looked wild. So she was still dancing while he was talking, still wiggling and dancing. I didn't know that was his wife but he told me, say, "That's my wife." Cold, black, ugly gal, with her hair all kinky up on her head— oh Lord! She wasn't tending to nothing. And her body, you could smell her body all across the place every time she danced. All this was killing me, you know, 'cause that was all my people all around in there against the woman too. So anyway, when he said that was his wife I pitied him, and was saying to myself, "Don't mess with him; don't fool with him; don't pay him no mind. This is death." But I wound myself up in him, then afterwards I went and talked with God, say, "Must I do it?" You know, I get the message from Him 'cause it's His satisfaction and He did say, "Don't give my bread to the dog." But I'd done got wound up in him before he left me, though he didn't know it. He done something to me. It was his time's all. So anyway, I prayed with him.

Afterwards, we were getting ready for sleep and I thought it was all over with. So while I was in the room getting ready for bed somebody knocked on the door, said, "I just want you to put your hand on me and tell me you're praying for me." That was something! So then I called him on the inside, and sure enough I just went on and prayed with him. I talked with him and read with him and prayed with him. And he sit there; sometimes he shiver like in that funny way they do. Anyhow, he went on and told me, said, "From this night on I'll never put another needle in my arm." He pulled his sleeve up, and that thing got away with me! I say, "What you do there?" He said, "I'll never put another needle in my arm." He thought I knew, but I'd never seen nothing like that before. I say, "Father, man sticking needles in himself!" Lord, he needed help. I told him one thing to do to rebuke that sin, drive away evil spirits. I didn't tell him that night but I told him the next day how to keep them away from him, how to keep him from tagging with them all the time so he could handle himself a little better. Common things, but it's good; it's God. So I told him that and he said he would. Then he said would I talk to his wife too. So she came then. And so she came; she had on pants, clean clothes, and she looked well. She come for me to pray with her, and I talked to her good. I mean I talked to her, 'cause she had hurted me so much till I had to cry while talking to her. It was something to think about, you know. Being a woman, she had a long ways to go to help herself, even with that husband she had. "And since he's got a mind to come off what he's doing," I say, "you got to really stop to help him. If you don't it would be a low blow."

So we talked a long time. We talked about her home, and the child told me all about how she was brought up in a church, you know, and did work for the Lord and all of that, and how her father was a good Christian a long time before her mother was. And then her mother turned to be a Christian too. She say she won't let her brother know where she was at or nothing, on account that she was ashamed of the way she was living. That's right. And now you ought to see her!

So I left there, and instead of us coming home we went to Detroit. They had a little short program up there and we stayed a night and a day. But that boy left home the next morning, and told his momma, say, "I'm going home with Bessie. I'm going home with Bessie Jones and I'm going to stay with her a while." He thought I was coming home. And some way or another he got the money and came straight on to St. Simons while I was in Detroit, and somebody told my son that someone was looking for me and I wasn't there. And so George went there and met this young man, and he told him he was looking for me to pray with him 'cause he needed help. He'd been wanting to go back into the dope, you know. And George just took his bag and put it in the house and they kept right on down to the church and they stayed right there. Mattie—George's wife—got some more people to come down later and they prayed with him. Afterwards, he stayed with George. And this woman, she called to ask was I there, 'cause whe wanted to know where her son was, to be sure that he hadn't got killed or nothing had happened to him. And he was there but I wasn't there so George talked to her.

About two weeks ago while I was sitting out on the porch, two white ladies come up in a car and one said, "I know you don't know me but I know you through my son." She was the same woman, the mother. I didn't know her. Then she told me her son was a minister now. He's a minister! And she said, "I got me the prettiest chocolate grandbaby you most ever seen." Yeah, him and the girl are still together and they got a baby now. Oh, I felt so good! I was just glad. The Lord put me and my son together, and that one step made it. "I shan't give up."

But see, that boy saw himself among the living and was dead, not fitted for nothing but to be cut down and drug out. And when you get that way, something comes to strike you and God has something for you, too. God did it to him right there, that's all. And you see them trees out there, they don't be thinking about nobody dead walking off sometimes, that root will come up and spread out, be one of the prettiest trees you ever did see. That's the mighty Lord, had a change in me. He said, "I'm going to build you a second time, and this time you shall be built." And I was telling how I could just see myself; you know how you take the second time to fix something up that be trying to live at the bottom but the top don't look good at all. Like you're about to die, see, but the bottom is still trying to live; the root is still there. You got the word in you but you ain't using it. See what I'm talking about? That's what I mean. And see, I was telling them about that. I had asked God to help me live: don't let my root die. Don't turn against me! That's what I was asking the Lord. And when I did that, I could see myself. I could just see myself coming again and I was born again. And that boy could see himself too. He could see himself too in that way.

The lady offered me money, you know, but I told her I didn't need any money 'cause that was God's work. But she said, "If ever you need anything, any time, call on me." She was just so happy she didn't know what to do. Said she goes where she wants to now and she feels alright. Feels good. Course she wasn't no Christian, but she wasn't no dope addict either. She was a fine, healthy woman, she seemed to be. And you know, you never know sometimes. You just can't throw folks away.

And a girl came to me a few weeks ago—she stays on the Island—and she was in bad shape. I've known her since she was a baby. She came over to my house about three Sundays ago while I was getting ready for church, and she wanted me to pray for her right there. So we stayed there and prayed and prayed and prayed, and I didn't get to church that day. I mean, she was all on the floor, she was every which-a-way. She was just praying.

She was there. And so she went through a great change and I thank God for it. What got it though, I told her, say, "The devil's going to pick at you. He'll sure pick at you, and if you're not sharp he'll get you 'cause that's his job. He don't want to worry you now while he's got you, see. But after you go to leave, that's when he wants you." Sure enough, that same night we seen her about drinking again. She says, "Yeah, I'm drinking again." I said, "All those bottles and things laying around, just throw them away." She said the devil told her she'd done wrong, see. But she's holding up now, holding up beautifully. Her husband said she ain't touched none in a while, ain't took another lick. And he comes home to a clean house and his food is ready. That's a great change. I told her, say, "You ain't got to come to our church, go any place you want to, but wheresoever you go, go with Jesus. Let the Lord lift you up and be strong. That's all."

Naturally, every church up under heaven should be clean. We call it a church but where you worship God at, the place should be clean. Course you ain't going to find one that's wholly clean—mine or nobody else's—'cause Satan must be in there some way, somehow. Regardless of what you do, he's going to have his part. He walked with Jesus Christ; you know he's going with you. I don't care how much religion you got, the devil's gonna stick with you too. He gonna try to make you look back. Some folks say, "You got religion, so why you got to pray?" But that's why you got to pray! Makes me sick 'cause people don't see into it like they ought to. When they want something to slur and talk about they say, "I don't pray that much and I know I ain't got no religion." I say, "You don't? Then you ain't got nothing to pray for." You got to pray to keep this thing. Just like living with your wife or husband, you got to live right to keep it. You got something, you better try to take care of it. Jesus says your momma may have it, your poppa may have it, but blessed is he who has something of his own. 'Cause Momma and Poppa sure can't save you.

I love it, not just because my grandparents brought me up to do these things. Many others brought up the same way I was are gone on about their business because it didn't stick with them.

Like throwing water on a duck's back. But my grandparents helped me to get saved. They brought me up in a way that I could see it and that helped me a whole lot. When I pray with you, I can't save you but I can help you see the light and understand. Obey God's word and you get right in it, 'cause God knows all things and can save anybody. Some say, "My daddy prayed for me long years ago," or "My momma prayed for me and I was baptized when I was a baby." And it hurts me. That baptism you had then, that was just sprinkling water on the skin and them clothes. God don't want you to be baptized that way nohow. But a lot of folks got it in their mind that they don't need any more. That's backwards. That's way off. But a lot of folks are depending on that and it's pitiful, 'cause the devil gets you wrapped up that way. So that's what it means. You tell the person the way they ought to go, but they got to count their own steps, step by step, and do the right thing to keep from turning this way or that. They got to have strength to do it their own self. A woman can sit down and make you a dress but she can't wear it for you.

Yet God said, "Trust in me and I will open up doors for you." It's wonderful. You trust and God will pour out blessings to you so you won't be able to receive all of them. Therefore you must have a giving heart, and know what to do with it to help others. Not in the way that the devil shows, like that Reverend Ike. He's showing the folks how they can get I done forgot how many Cadillacs and everything like that, but that don't carry you nowhere but here. 'Cause you're gonna die and leave every bit of it right here. And if you're underminded and got it, that's just your bad luck. If you didn't trust God first, then that's your bad luck. And all that giving people numbers, and all that kind of thing, I don't see any sense to it.

My momma's dead and gone, and I don't know whether it was God or who it was, but when she said, "I need me some so-and-so; I sure need to take me a number," that woman would see that number. And whatever it was, she played it straight. Some folks say turn it around or play it upside down, but Momma say, "Uh, uh. I see so-and-so and that's what I'm going to play." She'd go right on and play it and it would hit. I just laughed at that. She'd say, "I don't know when I'll get another; when I get in bad shape, I guess." Well that made me think God did it. I believe the Lord gives you just what he wants you to have.

I get a lot of satisfaction out of teaching and I do believe it was my calling. That's why I have to do it as a favor, you know. I pray and ask God to give me what he believes I should have, and place me where he wants me to be. And see, whatsoever it is that he gives me to do, I'm successful with that. And I ain't going to try to do nothing else. I ain't going to try to make myself no more and I ain't going to try to climb no hill or nothing unless he push me up there. God has been good to me, that's why I've never had to study about singing with people. On the programs when I'm leading the songs and games, I do it according to the congregation. I don't mean to size. There might be a hundred people there and they don't sound well because the spirit isn't working right. It feels just like you're in a place you're not welcome and the quicker you get out, the better it would be for you. And it's usually right there where it's needed. I'm going to pour out my spirit right there and here we go! That's God. You just work directly with Him and He'll work with you. Then you don't worry about what you're going to do because He's going to do it. And it'd be the same if you were singing a song or talking to people. He'd fall right in there and tell you just what to do, then you just go right on. Don't take it on your own, 'cause "without me, you can do nothing." I know some folks write down what they're gonna do and then read it while they're talking, but I just don't see it being done that way. 'Cause see, the gun isn't loaded. And you can't be loading it yourself and unloading as you go along. Momma used to say sometimes a man in the field with one of them jackass mules holler, "Gowee, gowee!" The mule had that man thinking he said, "Go preach! Go preach!" Thought he heard God talking. A lot of people are that way: they're just gone.

I heard a man say one day he got in hard luck in Florida, couldn't get no money nowhere and he'd always been too scared to steal. He just couldn't find a way out. So one day—it had to be the devil—a voice says to him, "Go on and be a preacher." He had a good education and knew all them hard words and everything, so he got him a good Bible and went to walking door to door telling people about Jesus. He had a good voice and the tongue for it; the devil gave him that good sound and everything, so he went on and was a preacher. He made himself some good money. And when he did, he forgot about it and went and got himself a great big bar. He was sitting there with his table full of liquor and just doing it big. One night he went home and some of the folks caught him. Wasn't he the same man who had been preaching to them against the ways of the devil? When they started beating and knocking on him with ". . . and you called yourself a preacher!" he asked God to help him. But the voice said, "Good sir, he didn't help you do it; you better run!" He said he got out from there! See, he went to playing with preaching and almost got himself killed. Lots of people do things on "self," but when you go for self you're wrong. If you try to do something do it right, because the devil's got so much he can teach you although it ain't nothing more than trying to prank with God. That's what I think about it. 'Cause if you're working for the devil and working for him right he's gonna show you many points and many things although ain't none of them good. He's something like a pacifier in a baby's mouth, the devil is. He always got something for you to suck on but nothing for you to feed on. And when you find out, when you know anything, you still hungering and thirsting after righteousness. Your soul is empty. Then when he pulls that pacifier out, you ain't got nothing and you can't get nothing. He's the first one to laugh at you. But he always got something to offer you.

Now with me coming from the outside, I think I brought something good to the music on the coast. I feel they know that what they're doing now with me, they would have never done without me. I feel they know that definitely. I mean they wouldn't have carried it on in the old way like it's supposed to be done, and they wouldn't have had the feeling of the old people who first begun these songs—what brought them out under hardships, and crying-ship, and suffering. And God handed it down to them in the midst of all the moaning and groaning. Well they might have sung the old songs—a lot of them are singing them now but they're carrying them to different tunes, and they're cutting them up this way and that way. But I like it just straight, you know. To carry it like I learned it, how old things go in places, not just Dawson and Fitzgerald but other places and with churches and things. The old folks everywhere had that same good feeling, and spiritual minds, and deep thoughts. And you could see into it that they meant it. There were hard pressure things that came over them, you know, and they weren't doing this here to just say they were singing. They were doing it to help their feelings, to help their spiritual lives. And the things within them was singing. They weren't just trying to be heard, to be seen, the spirit within them was crying out, was singing the grievances and whatnot. And that makes a difference. Every one of those old songs when done right is different. There are real differences in the tunes, a difference in how they're supposed to be carried.

On TV and PTL some of them are hitting these old songs we used to sing, but not in the same spirit. Ain't nothing to what they do, nothing extra to it. Ain't nothing much in it, no deep feelings. The Lord said he's gonna appoint a spirit upon all flesh and then all sons and daughters shall prophesy. And that's true. He's doing it. 'Cause He said, before He let the devil have more souls than Him, He'd make souls out of stone. He didn't mean rocks: that means stony-hearted people who wouldn't bow, stony-hearted people who wouldn't yield. I used to hear white folks praying, when they called themselves praying or talking to the Lord, and they didn't hardly ever say anything about Jesus. I told a white man that once at our house. I said, "You white people, you figure 'cause you're white and you're so high and have money and everything else in the United States and other places too in your hands, you figure that you don't talk to that little boy, you talk to God." Everything they say, they say "Oh God!" But Jesus said, "You got to come in by me," you see. And now you can hear them talking to Jesus. The son of the living God. Now you can hear them doing that, see. So they come in that way, and they're singing the same old songs and they're doing what the Lord said, "I will place into your mouth a new song." And so, even though there ain't much in the way they do, it sounds just as good to them as the old songs sound to us. And they sing about "Lift him up until he speaks from eternity," and they got so much stuff in there till I wouldn't hardly know it if I hadn't heard them say the words. But yet and still, God ain't gonna lie. "I will place into your mouth a new song." And so let it come that way. Then go right back and don't forget the old path. And when you find it, walk therein. Don't forget the old path. I can sing all these new songs; I can sing right along with them—those that I know—but I just don't forget the old path.

If the Lord hadn't let me have the knowledge and the under-standing to bring in these yard games and songs like we did long years ago, and get them on record, they would have already run out somewhere. They would have, 'cause at some schools the teachers sing some of the same things we did but it's way off. It's different. And when she was in New York Mabel Hilary had them children playing my games—she knew the right way—but she had them in her way. In "Little Johnny Brown" she had them get down on their knees to fold the blanket. And I spoke about that onstage. I said I was glad to see the children come to know the games that Mabel had taught them, 'cause Lomax had al-ready told them on the stage that they were my games. I said I was glad to see that she was keeping them up but that I didn't have any lazy Johnny Brown. I had never seen anyone get on their knees to play Johnny Brown before. And in the "Aunt Dinah" game there wasn't any skipping, no zest. The verses were given out like hymns:

> Way down yonder in an old cornfield
> Blacksnake popped me on my heel
> Pop my whip I run my best
> I run my head in a hornet's nest
> I'm goin' away to see Aunt Dinah
> I'm goin' away to see Aunt Dinah

and they walk away but no tune. Not that much tune. A funny tune. But see, it was just out of the way. It was what you call modern. The modern style. They're changing to stay up with the times but that just makes it go away. You wouldn't know where it went, wouldn't know where it came from.

I hear a lot of young people singing gospels—what they call gospel—and I don't feel any particular way about that. I do like for the young people to sing spirituals. But I don't feel any particular way about gospel, not if they name it that, 'cause gospel ain't nothing but gospel—I don't care where it comes from and how it goes—and I think they should preach the gospel and sing spiritual songs and jubilee songs and do it that way. That's what I think. And when they're singing and putting all that stuff in it, like ". . . and you know what? I'll tell ya . . .," I don't like that. But I just take it. That's their way of doing it. And I just sit up there and listen at it and go on. But that's their way. I ain't never told them to stop it 'cause they ain't singing for me, but I don't think it fits; it's not natural. I sure don't think it fits. But everybody's got their own way, and you sure have to sing spirituals and jubilee songs and hymns and zions. Now zion songs are good. A lot of people don't realize it but zion songs are very slow. Jubilee songs are fast. Spirituals are either fast or slow. We sing spirituals. A lot of the gospel songs that are sung these days are fast, and they put all kinds of things in there I don't think they should, but God knows their heart. That's the main thing.

And a lady asked me one day, she said, "You don't sing blues?" I said, "Not with this. I been quit singing them things many years now." "And no love songs?" I said, "Oh yes sir." She drew up, "Oh, you sing love songs?" I said, "Yeah." And she asked, "What's the difference?" I said, "There's a lot of difference, because I sing love songs to Jesus." I said, "Every one of the songs I sing is a love song." I couldn't sing a love song years ago, because I wasn't singing love. I was just singing wishing songs, and good-time songs; backyard blues wishing you were this way or that way or this place or that place. And wishing you could be with somebody you ain't with and all that kind of stuff. Wasn't no love in it at all. And hatred songs, where you call people all sorts of names. You could make up any kind of a song you want to with that; I could. I used to could. But when you sing a love song you're going the straight way; it's going to be about the Lord; it's going to be about your soul. I said, "All I sing now is love. That's all I do." And I just hushed her mouth right off me because the way she had it was otherwise—wishing songs, the desire to do this, to do that, instead of singing love of it. My granduncle was a guitar picker and he used to sing those songs too. Anything he wanted. And when his lady quit him he used to sing to get her back. He'd sing a song and make it. And there was a girl up there named Leola who was a great dancer. Then she came to be a sporting woman and they made a song about her, "Leola is about to run me crazy." That's those desire songs. They were telling the truth their own way, "I'm going home to get my razor, coming back and kill my baby," and all like that. They were right on it. Same way it is about Christ: you'd be right on it.

I went to a church not too long ago, and wasn't a Bible in there. The preacher, he brought me home, and he said he had over three hundred members but all they talked about in that church was themselves, about the nature of the earth, about the cows, and rocks, and mountains. But who put it there? Who put the breath in the cow, who grew the grass? They ain't got that background. Who blows the wind? They get nothing about that. To me that teaching ain't worth a dime. It's just a way to make money. The preacher said that if he went to telling them how they ought to live, he wouldn't have a church. I said, "But you will have a bunch of hell to get in, because the Lord wants you to tell the people the truth. If you don't tell them the truth, you and they are going to be buckled together, because they're going to try to beat the devil out of you for fooling them." And we've seen that in the prophecies: the men and women hanging, moaning and groaning, and when the meaning was told, it was these were the false prophets that were teaching the people the wrong way. That were them and their disciples.

Everybody is a disciple of something, and anything you're a member of, that's what you get paid for. You can turn your head, or get drunk, or kiss a bear if you want to; it doesn't matter. As long as you've not paid you're in debt. But Jesus said you must be born again, and if you're born in the spirit you're going to do right. That's all there is to it, that's why we don't have a preacher. We don't pay a preacher to preach, that's crazy. That's wrong all over the world; I don't care who does it. And I tell them that in their own churches—I don't go up in their pulpits because I don't have any business there—but I tell them it's wrong to pay a preacher. It says go without stripe, without coat, without anything, and I will pay your rewards. And you pay your tithes and give your offerings. If you pay your tithes, God will make your job so good! If you pay your tithes God will make your health so good. God would open up doors and windows you never thought about. You know, the worse old cracker walking the street will pay his tithes. He pays, because he wants that blessing. You could be a drunkard, a liar, a gambler or murderer, if you pay your tithes, God will pay you 'cause He ain't gonna shun his word. He didn't say I'll send you to heaven if you pay, but I'll open doors down here for you. But you got to pay that ten percent. I don't care who you are, you're getting. And when you give, give it directly from your heart and mean it. It won't get you to heaven necessarily, but it sure will keep you out if you don't do it. That's the truth, so help me.

And I've been to many places, schools and such, and wherever I go I teach it. I teach the word, because that's all they need—the word. It's all in me and it's all I'm going by—the word. The word was sent me. I asked God to give me something to do to come out of myself, that I could do something for somebody and do something good. All my people are dying and going, and nobody's leaving anything. Don't even have land to leave—although the land doesn't do any good since the cracker will take it. Too many of us die and don't leave what we know. Mr. Julius, my stepdaddy, he could make tombstones, he could make fans and other beautiful things. I said, "Mr. Julius, teach it to me." He said, "No. The white folks might arrest me if I do." And he never did teach it.

Things have changed a whole lot so nowadays people don't have to sing songs at anybody. People sing now for their own benefit and joy, except maybe for blues singers and stage singers that sing against one another. I'm not talking about myself, because I sing the old-time songs and they can come if they want to or they can let it alone. I'm right there and I ain't moving, because that's all I want to do. But most of the songs now, they just make them up, just trying to make something new, something different. And we get some that ain't no song at all.

I get lots of satisfaction out of my music, quite naturally, and other folks' music too, 'cause I just love music. But for myself, it's great to me when I'm singing and can think to myself that I'm singing something I need to sing. And I think to myself when I'm singing something that my old foreparents and the other folks of that tribe along in those days knew, that if their spirits came around me, I believe they would be rejoicing. They would know it; they would say, "That's the song that we used to sing." What we have to understand is that they're here all the time. Not yesterday or tomorrow, but all the time. And as long as they're around me, I believe they'd be happy.

# Bio-Chronology

| | |
|---|---|
| February 8, 1902 | Bessie Jones born in Smithville, Ga. |
| | Attended the Mountain Grove school/church in Dawson, Ga. |
| September 15, 1914 | Birth of first child (daughter), Osierfield, Ga. |
| 1915 | Became farmhand in inland Georgia. |
| June 11, 1919 | First trip to St. Simons Island. |
| 1920 | Returned to inland Georgia, continued work as farmhand. |
| September 20, 1924 | First trip to Florida. Spent nine years here. |
| August 28, 1929 | First met George Jones. |
| July 1932 | Joined Church of God in Christ. |
| August 27, 1932 | First baptism. |
| 1933 | Settled in St. Simons Island with George Jones. |
| 1933 | Joined Lydia Parrish's Coastal Georgia Spiritual Singers Society. |
| August 25, 1935 | Birth of second child (son), St. Simons Island |
| December 26, 1937 | Birth of third child (son), Brunswick, Ga. |
| 1938 | Worked with the crops in Maryland. |
| 1939 | Began work as domestic on St. Simons Island. |
| Spring 1954 | Met Alan Lomax. |

| | |
|---|---|
| 1954 | Singing engagements in Berkeley and Los Angeles, Cal. |
| 1954 | First record made with Alan Lomax. |
| 1954 | Sang at Carnegie Hall, New York City. |
| 1955–65 | First movie made with Alan Lomax (1955). |
| | Many concert, campus, and festival appearances, including Central Park, New York City, and Newport, R.I., 1965. |
| 1966–75 | Continued campus, concert, and festival appearances, including Folk Life Festival, Washington, D.C.; Mariposa Festival, Toronto, Canada; U.S. Pavilion, Montreal, Canada. |
| | Also *Yonder Comes Day* (movie); *Step It Down* (book). |
| 1976— | President Carter's inauguration, Washington, D.C. |
| | Continued concert, campus, and festival appearances, plus workshops at various public schools, including Fresno, Cal., Boston, Mass., Brunswick, Ga., and Los Angeles, Cal. |
| July 3, 1982 | Awarded a National Heritage Fellowship by the National Endowment for the Arts at the annual Folklife Festival in Washington, D.C. |

# Photographic Essay

The headtie and apron worn by former generations of black women and retained as costume pieces in performance of the spirituals are widely rejected by younger black females today. Such garments evoke the disliked image of the black mammy, and they refuse to wear them in performance, preferring their natural hair or in some cases wigs. Among older heads like Bessie a sharp distinction is made between the self and its image. Consequently, although in later years she adopted the wig for public performances, Bessie sees nothing wrong with wearing traditional costume if that is what it takes to maintain patronage of the music. In a moment of ease and candor, she is quite comfortable without either wig or headtie.

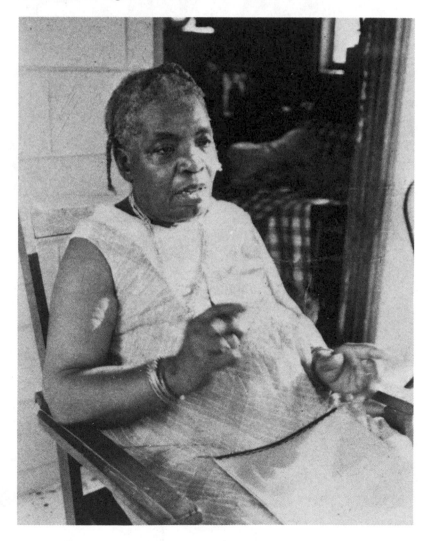

When she organized the Spiritual Singers Society of Coastal Georgia, Lydia Parrish noted how central "singing families" were in maintaining the style and repertoire of the spiritual tradition. But "singing families" are not just the result of some genetic connection. Singers are made as well as born, and the family is a context for both the donation of talents and the fostering of skills. Here Bessie is singing with some of her grandchildren while waiting for a train. These and others of her grands and great-grands have performed with her on stage across the country. She hopes that some of them will follow her in giving full commitment to the tradition.

As mother, grandmother, and great-grandmother, Bessie enjoys the company of the children. Her childhood relationships with parents and grandparents is a warm and cherished memory. And in relationships with her offspring she has tried to be to them as her parents were to her. At performances, at functions, or while taking a meditative stroll along the beach at St. Simons she is seldom without young companions. Such companionship is a context not only for instruction in songs, texts, and song-game dances, but also the manner in which the surrounding world is to be perceived, understood, and addressed.

Continuity for the Georgia Sea Island Singers as a performing group is increasingly centered on Douglas Quimby. Various circumstances including his gifts as a singer, his commitment to the tradition, and Bessie's approval of his musical and social personality coincide to bring Doug and the leadership role together. Like Bessie, Doug is from inland Georgia. His induction into the coastal performing tradition followed marriage to Frankie Quimby, formerly the daughter-in-law of Bessie Jones. Together Bessie, Doug, and Frankie form the heart of the current Georgia Sea Island Singers.

When listening to spirituals being sung it is easy to forget that the lives out of which they come were forged in an atmosphere of pervasive violence and terror. The whipping and mutilation of plantation slavery and the lynching after emancipation were prime expressions of that violence, and the spiritual world of blacks is read in part as a countervailing invention to the brutality and terror of their real circumstances. But there was terror in the spiritual world too. On a return visit to Dawson, Bessie stands smiling on the porch of this now abandoned house. But as a child here she had the experience of seeing a young man who had been babysitting with her shot. He had set her aside and walked off the porch to receive the bullets from another black man who had vowed his death following an argument. The young man's ghost returned to the scene frequently during the family's stay in this home, according to Bessie.

In the old yard at Dawson Bessie found the vines and the fruit with which as a child she had played "maypop."

Later she had an acquaintance collect some special dirt that is not available on St. Simons. The ingestion of dirt (geophagy) for its healing properties, especially by pregnant women, is a long-held trait within black folk culture. That special dirt joins honey, apple vinegar, moss, and various herbs in the medical kit of knowledgeable folk homes. It is also an old folk style to collect and store herbs and other remedies in advance of need, either for themselves or for others who may call on them for help with certain ailments.

In Dawson Bessie visited the library that she could not have used as a child because of segregation. The librarian welcomed her as an acclaimed daughter of the region and asked her to autograph library copies of a previous publication. With a characteristic largesse of spirit Bessie complied. Later in the year she was invited back to the library for a performance. This was important to her, inasmuch as it was the first time she had performed as a professional in this area of her childhood.

Coastal Georgia is replete with structural reminders of the plantation era, which coastal writers and historians remember as a time of gallantry, daring, industriousness, and romance. Slavery is recalled as a benign and humane institution in which slaves were regarded as members of the masters' households. Here at one end of St. Simons this ruin is marked as that of a slave hospital maintained by one of the leading plantation families. Its walls are made of tabby—a durable mixture of sand, lime, and oyster shells. At the opposite end of the island the cabin attests to the kind of dwelling in which the slaves lived and which continued as a dwelling long after slavery had ended.

Harvesting the sea and inland waterways is a ubiquitous activity along the coast. People fish at all hours of the day or night. Shrimping is an industry; crabs, oysters, and clams are also harvested in abundance. Some black fishermen own their boats and work the coast as far away as Virginia or Texas. Others prefer to cast from land. Here at the St. Simons festival this netmaker demonstrates his craft. He is weaving a casting net—a one-man net that is cast from shore. Black craftsmen have been making such nets for generations and the craft is usually maintained within a family.

There is no family tradition associated with manufacturing crab traps, however. This is a simple but ingenious device made from chicken wire. A small box containing the bait is hung inside the outer frame. A telescoped entrance allows the crabs to squeeze in after the bait but prevents their getting out.

In the old days, before bridges to the mainland and well-developed road systems on the island, sea islanders took themselves around on the water. One of the "oldest" song forms developed by slaves in the region was the rowing song—a subgenre in the general repertoire of work songs.

Among the more popular work songs from the region are those associated with the planting and harvesting of rice. While the sea islands became famous for their cotton, rice was also an important plantation crop for the coastal region. The town of Riceboro was the center of a once thriving rice-growing area. Some distance south of Riceboro is the Altama plantation. The fields are dry now, and the outlines of the paddies are all that mark their previous existence. But the plantation is maintained as a family heirloom, and the Georgia Sea Island Singers regularly perform their traditional repertoire of songs there. The mortars, pestles, basket, and tarp are all associated with the coastal rice culture and are used in the work-song performances.

The peanut was and continues to be a major inland crop, and there are traditional work songs associated with the harvest here too. But as is true for many similar instances, the songs become lost when agricultural systems change. Much peanut farming is mechanized, but after the tractors pull the roots out of the earth the pods are still removed by hand. When Bessie saw these young ladies picking peanut pods in front of a mound of roots, she joined them to show how the picking was done in her day—with song. They had never heard such a song and were alternately skeptical and delighted by her rendition.

When she was "in the world," Bessie did her share of fast living. She partied and frolicked and kept beat with the blues. But this was only to be a passing phase for her and eventually she was called to a change. She rediscovered religion and helped to found this church on St. Simons, where her eldest son now serves as pastor.

The new life for her also involved a shift from migrant worker to stage performer. After being discovered by Alan Lomax, she played in a film made by him at Williamsburg—the restored colonial capital of Virginia.

As a performer Bessie has sung not only with her group, the Georgia Sea Island Singers, but has shared the stage with other performers as well. Here she is seen with Hubbart Smith at a concert in Chicago.

Performing could involve an informal moment of levity, too. Here Bessie shares such a moment with Gene Bluestein, folk musician and folklorist at the California State University, Fresno.

Bessie will sing anywhere, for anyone—at a senior citizens' center in California, at the campus of the University of Illinois, at a Boston elementary school—because the music and her talent for rendering it are gifts passed on to her from the Supreme through the ancestors. They are not individual properties to be sheltered and mined only for personal gain but gifts to be shared as freely as they were received. Besides, music is healing, it is motivating, it expresses and is a vehicle for the enduring relationship between man and maker. But it would not be any of these things if it were not freely performed.

Bessie will sing for anyone, but her love is for the children. This scene has been enacted countless times in her career, at schools, playgrounds, and other venues across the country from Georgia to Massachusetts to California, her voice raised with those of the children, her hands keeping time with the tambourine.

After Bessie, responsibility for maintaining the Georgia Sea Island Singers, the group's traditional repertoire, and its performance style devolves, on Doug and Frankie Quimby. They have been chosen—Doug the leading performer and Frankie the performer-manager. Their roles in respect to traditional culture have gone beyond their own stage appearances, too. Each year since 1977 they have directed the St. Simons Annual Folk Festival, which receives support from the National Endowment for the Arts, private donations, and the Glynn County Park District.

# Sources

## Selected Bibliography

Anonymous
    1972a Review of *Step It Down*. *Sing Out!* 21, no. 4: 29.
    1972b Review of *Step It Down*. *Journal of Music Therapy* 9, no. 4: 199.
    1974 Review of *Step It Down*. *American Music Teacher* 23, no. 4: 42–43.
Bluestein, Gene
    1977 "From the Ivory Tower: Folk Artists in the Universities." *Sing Out!* 26, no. 2: 18–20.
Carawan, G.
    1964 "The Living Folk Heritage of the Sea Islands." *Sing Out!* 14, no. 23: 28.
Cate, Margaret Davis
    1979 *Our Todays and Yesterdays*. Spartanburg, S.C.: Reprint Company.
Clark, Jim, ed.
    1964 *The Folk Music Yearbook of Artists*. Fairfax, Va.: Jandel Productions International, Ltd.
Fancher, Betsy
    1971 *The Lost Legacy of Georgia's Golden Isles*. New York: Doubleday & Co.
Foote, Bud
    1973 "Georgian Recalls Childhood Games." *Atlanta Constitution*, May 28: C8.
Harris, Art
    1974 "Sea Island Singer Preserving the Songs of Slave Days." *Atlanta Constitution*, Nov. 14: 5–13.

Hickerson, Joseph
    1965 "Alan Lomax's 'Southern Journey': A Review-Essay." *Ethnomusicology* 9, no. 3: 313–22.
Jones, Bessie, and Bess Lomax Hawes
    1972a *Step It Down: Games, Plays, Songs, and Stories from the Afro-American Heritage.* New York: Harper and Row.
    1972b "Teach In: Children's Games." *Sing Out!* 21, no. 4: 12–13.
Martin, Judith
    1970 "Slave Spirituals on the Mall." *Washington Post*, July 4: 61–62.
New York Times
    1972 "Yale University presents Duke Ellington Medal to 30 black musicians, among them Bessie Jones; several groups perform." Oct. 9, 36: 1.
Parrish, Lydia
    1942 *Slave Songs of the Georgia Sea Islands.*
Rhodes, Willard
    1973 Review of *Step It Down. Ethnomusicology* 17, no. 3: 49–50.
Sandberg, Larry, and Dick Weissman
    1976 *The Folk Music Sourcebook.* New York: Alfred A. Knopf.
Sutton-Smith, Brian
    1973 Review of *Step It Down. Journal of American Folklore* 86, no. 341: 307–8.
Tracey, Hugh
    1972 Review of *Step It Down. African Music* 5, no. 2: 118.
Wilson, J. S.
    1971a "Review of concert with B. Burk." *New York Times*, Jan. 10, 71: 1.
    1971b "Review of Philadelphia Folk Festival. Bessie Jones and others perform." *New York Times*, Aug. 31, 40: 4.
    1972a "Review of gospel singers. B. Jones concert at Our Lady of Peace Church under auspices of NY Pinewood Folk Music Club." *New York Times*, Apr. 16, 49: 2.
    1972b "Phila. Folk Music Festival revd. B. Jones (and others) perform." *New York Times*, Aug. 29, 23: 1.

## Discs

*American Folk Songs for Children*
Atlantic 1350, © 1954
Southern Folk Heritage Series

*Deep South—Sacred and Sinful*
Prestige/International 25005
Southern Journey Series

*Sources*

*Georgia Sea Islands, Vol. I*
Prestige/International 25001
Southern Journey Series

*Georgia Sea Islands, Vol. II*
Prestige/International 25002
Southern Journey Series

*Georgia Sea Island Songs*
New World Records NW 278, © 1977

*So Glad I'm Here: Songs and Games*
*from the Georgia Sea Islands*
Rounder Records 2015, © 1975

*Step It Down*
Rounder Records 8004

*Traditional Music at Newport, Part 1*
Vanguard VRS-9182, © 1965

*What a Time*
Southern Grass Roots Revival Project, © 1980

## Films

*Music of Williamsburg*

*The Georgia Sea Island Singers*

*Yonder Come Day*

# A Note on the Author

BESSIE JONES was born into a "singing family" in Smithville, Ga., in 1902, and many of the song-games she still performs were learned at an early age. Her experience as a farmhand and migrant laborer took her out of central Georgia into "following the crops" between Florida and Maryland. Singing and performing were a natural part of life in the work camps. In 1933 she settled on St. Simons Island and there joined Lydia Parrish's Coastal Singers Society. She rapidly mastered the style and repertoire, and over the years emerged as a master exponent of the black coastal oral tradition. With the assistance of Alan Lomax she became a nationally known figure in the mid-1950s. In that same decade the Georgia Sea Island Singers was formed under her leadership, and she has made countless concert, campus, and festival appearances with this group since then, including a performance at the inauguration of President Jimmy Carter in 1976. At the 1982 Folklife Festival in Washington, D.C., she was presented with a National Heritage Fellowship award by the National Endowment for the Arts. Bessie Jones is co-author (with Bess Hawes) of an earlier book, *Step It Down* (Harper & Row, 1972), and is featured on a number of records. She is widely known as a folklorist, herbalist, and religious personality.

# A Note on the Editor

JOHN STEWART is an associate professor of anthropology at the University of Illinois. He is a graduate of California State University, Los Angeles (B.A.), the University of Iowa (M.F.A.), and U.C.L.A. (Ph.D.). His publications include two previous books, *Last Cool Days* (A. Deutsch, 1971) and *Curving Road* (University of Illinois Press, 1975), and other short works on black expressive culture.